The Rules That Rebels
Live By

Jeff Farnham

Jer. 32:17

The Rules That Rebels Live By

By
Jeff Farnham

Post Office Box 1099 • Murfreesboro, Tennessee 37133

To

Ron and Patti Williams of Hephzibah House,
Winona Lake, Indiana, whose tireless labors
since 1971 have brought about the rescue of
many troubled souls and the comfort and
recovery of many of their families.

Don and Wenda Williams of Believers
Baptist Church, Winona Lake, Indiana,
whose faithful shepherding since 1997
has grounded those who have been
rescued and sent them forth to
faithful Christian living.

Contents

Preface

If believers were to cite any group who doesn't live by the rules, it would be rebels. They break the rules of decency, honesty, integrity and sincerity "like them that remove the bound" (Hos. 5:10)—they just live lawless lives. Because rebels break the biblical rules of spiritual responsibility and the normal rules of social acceptance, we tend to believe they have no rules.

Paradoxically, rebels do live by rules; however, they are rules of their own that greatly differ from rules followed by submissive, honorable, God-fearing people. Truthfully, every man serves what he loves, and the rebels' "abominations [are] according as they [love]" (9:10). Often, rebels adhere more closely to their rules than many in the Bible-believing crowd stick to theirs. Their dedication to the rules of rebellious living is almost admirable, though they are aligned with a wrong cause.

In an attempt to identify those who are rebels in the biblical sense, the chapters of this book are devoted to illustrating the various rules that rebels live by as seen in the lives of biblical characters—some famous and some obscure—who lived by those rules. Obviously, some of the rebellious individuals in God's Word lived by more than one rule. Just as obviously, some rules were followed by more than one Scripture rebel.

I have drawn from my own experience as a rebel prior to my salvation on October 25, 1974, and have gleaned from my own study of the Scriptures in the past thirty-six years to write this book. Having lived myself by many of the rules that rebels live by—and since my salvation having worked to replace those rebel rules with God's rules—and having observed many others, saved and unsaved alike, who were living by rebel rules and are hoping to replace them with God's rules, I have attempted to cover the subject without neglecting pertinent examples and without redundancy.

As already indicated, strange as it may seem, rebels do come from both sides of the salvation coin. The majority of characters listed in this book are idolaters and pagans who lived out in bold fashion the rules of rebellion attributed to them. Likewise, in life and ministry, most of the rebels one encounters are unsaved souls who have no indwelling Holy Spirit. However, it is important to note that rebellion is often lodged in the hearts of people of faith and salvation. When a believer is in rebellion, he lives by the rules of his unbelieving contemporaries and takes on the deportment of one who is a faithless infidel.

As long as believers and unbelievers have lived on earth, rebellion has been a reality. "There is a generation," Agur said three thousand years ago in Proverbs 30:11–14, with curses for its parents, filth in its hearts and swords in its mouths. Rebellion has social, financial, familial, ecclesiastical and spiritual implications. The whole of creation is infiltrated with rebel philosophy.

This book will be useful to the pastor, the evangelist, the church planter, the educator, the businessman, the parent, the friend—indeed to any person who encounters others and wants to help them. My prayer is that many lives will be turned to righteousness as a result of the following study.

An unsaved rebel must first be saved by the blood of Jesus Christ before he can find victory over the rules of rebels.

Abandonment of a rule of rebellion will not make any man a Christian. Further, saved rebels must be repentant to the point of seeking God for the 'tearing down of their strongholds' (II Cor. 10:4), lest they merely turn over a new leaf and fall back into their rebellious ways when pressure comes or temptation arises.

What Every Rebel Wants

Every rebel wants connection
    To the blessings of the saint,
Wants to have a little color
    Of the Christian's brilliant paint,
Wants to taste a tiny morsel
    Of the manna—Heaven's bread,
Wants to whiff a sweet aroma
    Of the Christian's flower bed,
Wants to get a little favor
    Of the faithful child of God,
Wants to own a little portion
    Of the Christian's plot of sod,
Wants to keep a soft remembrance
    Of the pleasant path of grace,
Wants to wear the precious jewels
    Of the Christian's shining face,
Wants to feel the peace and comfort
    Of the Christian's restful way,
Wants to sing the psalms of beauty
    Of the Christian's hope-filled day,
Wants to join the celebration
    Of the throng of grateful saved,
Wants to gain some fleeting remnant
    Of the fellowship he's waived,
Wants to know the precious secrets
    Of the ones who know the Word,
Wants to hide beneath the shadow
    Of the Christian's loving Lord,
Wants and wants but ne'er possesses,
    Wants and wants without relief,
Wants and wants amid distresses
    Due to sin and unbelief.

            —Jeff Farnham, December 2008

1
Who Is a Rebel?

Quite honestly, every man, woman, boy and girl is a rebel due to the inborn nature of sin. Thankfully, however, God does not label all persons as rebels because of their rebel blood and tendencies. Rather, God classifies people as rebels, scorners, evildoers, transgressors, fools and abominations only when He is describing individuals and groups whose testimonies are wholly given over to rebellion. Ezekiel 2:1–10 is a classic Old Testament passage on the subject of rebels and rebellion, and from that portion, I will present an accurate biblical description of a rebel.

A Rebel Is a Habitual Transgressor

First and foremost, rebels are constant in their practice of sin and disobedience. Ezekiel 2:3 mentions the ongoing, generational aspect of rebellion in its reference to "a rebellious nation that hath rebelled against me: they and their fathers have transgressed against me, even unto this very day." God does not name a man (or a nation) a rebel because of isolated incidents or infrequent deeds. Israel was rebellious, not due to an idolatrous act here or there, but because of generations of idolatry. Israel was deemed a rebellious house, not resulting from uncommon situations of rejecting God's Word, but from constant disregard for and disdain toward the revelation of Jehovah through the prophets. By application, rebels are habitual transgressors who live and work and practice their transgressions as a lifestyle.

Illustrations of the fact that rebels are those who habitually disobey appear throughout the pages of Scripture. In Genesis, mankind became so corrupt over several generations that God destroyed the earth. In the history of the Hebrews under Moses, murmurings and complaints were the routine. In the days of the judges, the cycle of apostasy, servitude, repentance and deliverance was constantly repeated. Under the kings, Israel rebelled until it was customary to do so. The New Testament letters to the Corinthian assembly address diverse types of in-church rebellion that were normal in the society of the first century. The Book of Revelation speaks of the final world rebellion prior to the fleeing away of earth and Heaven and the Great White Throne Judgment. In all these cases, and in more that could be considered, rebellion was a tradition, a custom, a uniform characteristic of the whole.

A Rebel Is a Hardhearted Transgressor

As the Lord continued speaking to Ezekiel, he told him that the nation of Israel were "impudent children and stiffhearted" (2:4) and "impudent and hardhearted" (3:7). Regardless of specific terminology, rebels have intractable, impenetrable hearts where exists an unapproachability, a bar-rier to any type of correction, a stubbornness that cannot be reworked by the Master Potter.

God did not call David a rebel, even though David rebelled in lying, committing adultery and murder. One reason God did not assign the word *rebel* to David is that he was softheart-ed. When confronted with his own sins, David broke into sin-cere sorrow and contrition. His heart was tender to the woo-ing and moving of the Holy Spirit. Obviously to the contrary, Saul, before David, was a rebel, showing no God-inspired repentance or grace-motivated remorse but only grousing regrets when Samuel approached him about his sins. His rebellious heart was hardened to the gentle entreaties of the Spirit.

A Rebel Is a Heedless Transgressor

The next thing God told Ezekiel was that Israel was a nation of rebels because they would not listen to truth. In Ezekiel 2:5 and 7, the Lord used the clauses "whether they will hear, or whether they will forbear" to indicate that Ezekiel was to give God's truth regardless of their response. In both of these verses, God told Ezekiel what Israel's response would be through the words "for they are a rebellious house" and "for they are most rebellious." God explained this refusal to listen and attend to truth when He told Ezekiel that "the house of Israel will not hearken unto thee; for they will not hearken unto me" (3:7).

God clearly identified rebels as those who may hear truth with physical ears, but who never let those "sayings sink down into [their] ears" (Luke 9:44). A rebel is a hearer but not a doer of the truths he encounters. Heedlessness among rebels is obvious from God's statement in Proverbs 27:22: "Though thou shouldest bray a fool in a mortar among wheat with a pestle, yet will not his foolishness depart from him." This aspect of rebellion is also seen in the attitude of Jeremiah's hearers in Jeremiah 18:18: "Come, and let us smite him with the tongue, and let us not give heed to any of his words."

A Rebel Is a Haughty Transgressor

After covering the heedlessness of rebels, God told Ezekiel how haughty rebels are. In Ezekiel 2:6, God told the prophet not to be afraid of them, their words or their faces. He was warned that the rebellious house of Israel would seek to strike fear into the man of God through their arrogant countenances and impudent conversations. For that reason, God "made [Ezekiel's] face strong against their faces, and [Ezekiel's] forehead strong against their foreheads" (3:8). What reason would God have had to make his prophet's forehead "as an adamant harder than flint" (vs. 9) if these hearers were not haughty and huffy in their responses to the truths of the Word of God being delivered to them?

"Proud and haughty scorner is his name, who dealeth in proud wrath," wrote Solomon (Prov. 21:24). Later in his revelations to Ezekiel, God told the prophet about the sodomites, saying, "They were haughty, and committed abomination before me: therefore I took them away as I saw good" (Ezek. 16:50). Pride and haughtiness are to rebellion what atoms are to molecules in that the latter cannot exist without the former.

A Rebel Is a Hostile Transgressor

Ezekiel 2:6 uses word pictures of thorns, briers and scorpions to portray the type of treatment Ezekiel would receive at the hands of his hearers, the rebellious house of Israel. These words described the severity of persecution Ezekiel would need to endure as God's righteous mouthpiece in a day of apostate rebellion. Hostility is a trademark of rebels. They often resort to cruelty, harshness, injustice and malice to gain their ends and accomplish their goals.

In considering this, we are reminded of the hostility of Cain toward Abel, of Jezebel toward Naboth and of the Pharisees toward the Lord Jesus Christ. Their words were hostile; their actions were hostile; their helpers were hostile. Rebellion is usually carried out in a hostile environment. To the degree that rebellion prospers within a person's heart or a community or a nation, to that same extent, hostility thrives.

A Rebel Is a Harmful Transgressor

When the Lord cautioned Ezekiel, "But thou, son of man, hear what I say unto thee; Be not thou rebellious like that rebellious house" (2:8), He was warning Ezekiel of the harmful effect that the rebels could have upon him. Rebels are as adept at "soul winning," if not more adept, than believers are. God was admonishing Ezekiel not to give in to the temptation to become like the rebels to whom he had been called to give the truth.

The goal of rebels who cannot entrap the righteous in sin is to entice the righteous into starvation. For that reason, God went further in that verse and said, "Open thy mouth, and eat that I give thee." Ezekiel was to make the Word of God his sustenance and not allow himself to feed on the rebellious fodder of the culture around him.

There is a fable about a stork in a turkey yard that was beheaded for the holiday meal. While it does not come from inspired Scripture, God does teach the principle of harm by association. Had Ezekiel allowed the rebels of his day to convert him to their rebellion, he would have suffered the same harmful punishment they did. God warned Lot to flee Sodom "lest [he] be consumed in the iniquity of the city" (Gen. 19:15). The Lord said, "The rod of the wicked shall not rest upon the lot of the righteous" (Ps. 125:3).

A Rebel Is a Helpless Transgressor

God had commanded Ezekiel to eat what He gave him. That which God gave him was "a roll of a book," or a scroll, upon which was written the future of the rebellious house (Ezek. 2:9). The future of rebels is "lamentations, and mourning, and woe" (vs. 10). Unsaved rebels have no hope and are without God in this world. All rebels believe they are in control, and for a time God will allow their perverse ways. But eventually He will step into their lives, and they will have no helper in that day. In the day that God visits them, they will have no ability to control their lives, and God will do in them what He has sovereignly purposed to do.

The helplessness that ultimately visits rebels is indeed sad. They suffer the natural and spiritual consequences of rebellion until they can be heard to moan,

> "How have I hated instruction, and my heart despised reproof;
>
> "And have not obeyed the voice of my teachers, nor inclined mine ear to them that instructed me!"—Prov. 5:12, 13.

This sadness is the result of sowing rebellion, and the rebel must bear the full fruit.

A Rebel Is a Hypocritical Transgressor

Although they are loath to admit it, rebels know when a true spokesman of God has been among them. Their hypocrisy is in the very fact that they will not acknowledge what they know to be true. Notice that God told His prophet in Ezekiel 2:5 that whether or not they heard him, they would "know that there [had] been a prophet among them." All rebels know when a real Christian has stood up and carried the blood-stained banner of the cross and has refused to back down and quit. Their knowledge that a true messenger of God has been among them may come across as denial, and their recognition of God's man may be expressed as rejection. Their acknowledgment of God may be repressed by apathy that eventually leads to atrophy, but they still know.

Later, in Ezekiel 6:9, 10, the Lord said that when all the judgments and woes finally came upon them in their captivity, they would hate themselves for their stubborn stupidity and ridiculous rebellion, and they would know that God really was the Lord after all and that He had brought captivity and bondage upon them. In other words, rebels know at the time of hearing the truth that a man of God is among them, even though they hypocritically refuse to own up to it.

Furthermore, they know when the prophet's words come to pass that a true prophet has been among them, even though they often still maintain their hypocrisy in refusing to admit outwardly to it.

Who is a rebel, then? He is a habitual, hardhearted, heedless, haughty, hostile, harmful, helpless and hypocritical transgressor. His philosophy is abominable; his practices, reprehensible. The little good that he may occasionally accomplish is overrun by the tangled weeds and briers of a wild and uncultivated life that is not productive for Jesus Christ.

2
The Am-I-My-Brother's-Keeper Rule

*"Thus saith the LORD; For three transgressions of Tyrus, and
for four, I will not turn away the punishment thereof; because
they delivered up the whole captivity to Edom, and remembered
not the brotherly covenant."*

*"Thus saith the LORD; For three transgressions of Edom, and
for four, I will not turn away the punishment thereof; because he
did pursue his brother with the sword, and did cast off all pity,
and his anger did tear perpetually, and he kept his wrath for
ever."*—Amos 1:9, 11.

Brotherly love would surely be included in the biblical concept of "natural affection," and the violation of that blood-
related bond is a serious matter with God. One of the most pro-
found evidences of our pre-tribulation, last-days peril is the
covenant-breaking hatred that abounds in family and society all
around us (II Tim. 3:3). The rebels of our time, however, are not
the only ones who have forgotten and forsaken their brotherly
responsibility. Am-I-my-brother's-keeper rebellion was part of
the grave sin committed in Tyre and in Edom in the eighth century B.C., and it is evident in others in Scripture as well.

Cain

Am-I-My-Brother's-Keeper Sarcasm

Adam and Eve's firstborn son is mentioned sixteen times in

the fourth chapter of Genesis, and then once each in Hebrews, I John and Jude. His life's entire summary is a rebellion against God's infant revelation of the acceptable offering from those living in the post-Edenic, sin-cursed world. Long before there was any conflict within mankind due to overpopulation or national power struggles, two men engaged in what could properly be called World War One: Cain versus Abel.

Cain rebelled against God's distinct instruction regarding the offering, and when God did not receive his offering, Cain's countenance fell; that is, he became downcast with disillusionment and anger. Evidently, after God rebuked his self-made, bloodless offering, Cain and Abel talked, and Cain rose up against his younger brother and killed him.

John tells us that Cain was "of that wicked one," meaning that he was a child of the Devil, and that he slew Abel out of envy "because his own works were evil, and his brother's righteous" (I John 3:12). Jude adds to that indictment by pronouncing a woe, literally a judgment, against those who go "in the way of Cain" (Jude 11). Cain rebelled, first against God Himself, then against his God-given responsibility to his fellowman. As an unregenerate man, Cain rose up against righteousness, forfeited God's acceptance and reaped God's judgment.

Cain's am-I-my-brother's-keeper attitude shows him to be cynical and sarcastic. The fact that Cain would dare to tell God he did not know where Abel was and then ask, "Am I my brother's keeper?" (Gen. 4:9) reveals a rebellious impudence of grand proportion. The question that he posed to God seems to be, in essence and intent, Cain's sarcastic criticism of God's watch care. He as much as asked God, "Aren't You my brother's keeper? Haven't You done Your job?" Cain personifies this rule of rebels perfectly. The rank sarcasm of rebels who are called into account and drawn up short in face of their own shortsighted, ill-fated sins is nearly beyond belief.

Certainly Cain had no biblical responsibility or divine mandate to provide for Abel; he was as much an adult as Cain was. Abel's response to his obligation before God by bringing "a more excellent sacrifice than Cain" (Heb. 11:4) demonstrates that fact. Cain was, however, responsible to his brother in basic brotherly kindness. He obviously violated this by his murder of Abel and the subsequent pretense of not knowing what had happened. Aside from Adam and Eve, Cain was the first rebel outside the Garden of Eden, and he fostered a brand of rebellion seen many more times in Scripture.

Er and Onan

Am-I-My-Brother's-Keeper Selfishness

The biblical record of Genesis 38:7–10 states that Er and Onan, first- and second-born sons of Judah by his Canaanite wife, Shuah, were both slain by the Lord. This story adequately illustrates another aspect of the am-I-my-brother's-keeper rule of rebels. Er's wickedness is merely stated and not explained, leaving the reader of Scripture to wonder what he might have done that was so terrible as to merit such drastic intervention by the Lord. Onan's death at the hand of the Lord just three verses later is briefly explained as resulting from the fact that he would not raise up seed to his dead brother.

In a different way than Cain, he would not be his brother's keeper. He was obstinately selfish in his refusal to fulfill a responsibility his brother could no longer fulfill. He demonstrated his am-I-my-brother's-keeper selfishness by caring neither for his brother, nor for his brother's memory, nor for his brother's bereaved and burdened widow.

Onan's am-I-my-brother's-keeper rebellion involved his breaking of the brotherly covenant *after* his brother's death, just as Cain's involved his breaking of that covenant *before* and *in* his brother's death. Old Testament family responsibility is sketchy at best, but God's primal revelation to his patriarchal society obviously included the principle that Onan had a responsibility to marry his dead brother's widow and conceive seed with her so that she would have one to provide for her in her old age. The child of that conception would not be accounted to Onan, but to Er, enabling Er's name not to be blotted out.

Deuteronomy 25:5–10 gives further details of this duty. The passage provides an allowance that if a man chose not to fulfill this brotherly responsibility, he could appear before the elders, make his refusal public, endure public shame and live.

During the time when judges ruled, Boaz approached an unnamed relative, who was nearer of kin to Naomi and Ruth than he was, to let this unnamed man claim his inherited right to all that was Naomi's and Ruth's, but with the stipulation that he must raise up seed to Mahlon, the dead son of Naomi and husband of Ruth. When the unnamed family member realized that such an action would mar his own inheritance, he opted out, had his shoe loosed and relinquished the entire situation to Boaz, who then took Ruth as his wife. The first child of Boaz and Ruth was given to Naomi, who became his nurse, "and the women her neighbours gave it a name, saying, There is a son born to Naomi; and they called his name Obed" (Ruth 4:17).

Much later in Scripture, it was this brotherly responsibility that was cited and exaggerated by the Sadducees in their ridiculous story of the seven brothers who all had the same wife, each one dying childless (Matt. 22:24–27).

Regardless of the degree of God's expectation, it is clear that Onan understood what God had made known to his people in Genesis. Apparently, he had no problem with the marriage to Er's widow, but when it came to the fact that "Onan knew that the seed should not be his," he selfishly shirked "lest that he should give seed to his brother" (Gen. 38:9). The sudden death of Onan on this occasion shows that regardless of whether or not God's revelation is complete, man has a well-known, well-understood responsibility to his fellowman.

Cain pursued his living brother with the sword, and Onan cast off all pity to his dead brother. Each of them failed to keep the brotherly covenant, and each one suffered as a result of his am-I-my-brother's-keeper rebellion.

The Pharisees

Am-I-My-Brother's-Keeper Scorn

In the Ten Commandments, God told children to honor their parents, extending the application of the brotherhood concept to others within the family circle. But rebels feel no more responsibility to care for their parents than they feel to honor their siblings, because they presume that it is God's job to keep them. One of the many hypocrisies of the first-century Pharisees was the scorning of any "brother's keeper" responsibility toward parents. The Pharisees allowed their followers to neglect their aging, dependent parents by devoting money or property to the temple cause.

That the temple cause itself was corrupt was demonstrated when Jesus twice exposed its fraud by overturning the tables of the moneychangers and calling the place a "den of thieves" (Luke 19:46). These am-I-my-brother's-keeper rebels scorned the covenant responsibility to parents and approved of a system of dishonesty and dishonor.

In Mark 7:8–11, Jesus referred to their use of the word "Corban," an Old Testament word meaning "offering." If someone's parents needed help, he could tell them that his possessions were Corban, or dedicated to the temple. In this Pharisaic tradition, he was then forbidden to use it to help his parents, since it "belonged" to the temple. However, he was not actually obligated to turn it over to the temple. He could use it for himself; he was simply not allowed to give it to anyone to whom he had said it was Corban.

These am-I-my-brother's-keeper rebels felt that their arrival at a certain chronological age suddenly freed them from the Fifth Commandment. Jesus straightforwardly told them that they had laid aside and rejected the commandments of God through tradition.

Scripture squarely answers this rebellious attitude in I Timothy 5:4, 8:

> *"But if any widow have children or nephews, let them learn first to shew piety at home, and to requite their parents: for that is good and acceptable before God."*

> *"But if any provide not for his own, and specially for those of his own house, he hath denied the faith, and is worse than an infidel."*

Sharp words, these. Indeed, one would do well to heed the words of Scripture and avoid the rebellion of failure to be a brother's—or for that matter, a parent's—keeper. God is certainly the Keeper of the soul, but He charges each of us with the keeping of a brotherly love and a familial bond. Every person is responsible to do all within his power to keep his brothers as life necessitates. Doing so may mar someone's inheritance, but "a good name is rather to be chosen than great riches, and loving favour rather than silver and gold" (Prov. 22:1).

Think how differently the stories of Cain, Onan and the Pharisees might have turned out had they cared for their brothers and family members. Cain could easily have been a great hero of faith listed in Hebrews 11. Instead, he appears there as an example of what *not* to be. Onan could have had a story similar to that of Ruth and Boaz with Naomi had he cared to be his brother's wife's keeper. Rebels never leave behind good stories, but those who truly consider themselves the keepers of their own kinsmen can most definitely anticipate a reward for doing so.

Illustration

Consider the story of a disabled man and his wife. This couple had three sons and a daughter. Shortly after the children were of age, the wife passed away, leaving the husband dependent upon his children, none of whom cared for him. Their neglect became the gossip of the town, until one of the sons was confronted with the Gospel of Christ and was saved. God did an immediate work of grace, convicting this new believer of his am-I-my-brother's-keeper rebellion. He purposed to change his entire outlook regarding his father, much to the father's surprise and the siblings' mockery. So steadfast was this newly saved son's resolve, that he took out a second mortgage, remodeled his home to the convenience of his wheelchair-bound father and further added private living space for him. This son and his wife and their children were the sole caretakers for his father for nearly two decades until his death. Incidentally, they were also the sole inheritors of his estate, valued at nearly three-quarters of a million dollars!

The Rule That the Righteous Live By

Responsibility

The Bible gives many commands and precepts regarding the responsibility of man for man. Jesus clearly said, "Thou shalt love thy neighbour as thyself" (Matt. 22:39), and in the story of the Good Samaritan, He clearly defined who our neighbors are and how to be neighborly. This type of love that Jesus requires of the believer is clearly illustrated by the Holy Spirit, who said, "For no man ever yet hated his own flesh; but nourisheth and cherisheth it, even as the Lord the church" (Eph. 5:29). A man naturally nourishes and cherishes himself, so if he loves others as he loves himself, then he must love his neighbors with a love that nourishes and cherishes them.

James called the law of loving one's neighbor as oneself the "royal law" (Jas. 2:8) because of its noble intent and pure fruit. The righteous live by this royal law, the same rule that Paul said absolves every man of his debt to every fellowman:

> "Owe no man any thing, but to love one another: for he that loveth another hath fulfilled the law."
> "Love worketh no ill to his neighbour: therefore love is the fulfilling of the law."—Rom. 13:8, 10.

Once again, the love of neighbor as oneself is cited, and once again, the am-I-my-brother's-keeper rebel is seen as irresponsible toward his fellows.

The apostle John wrote, "And this commandment have we from him, That he who loveth God love his brother also" (I John 4:21). He also wrote, "We know that we have passed from death unto life, because we love the brethren," and, "Hereby perceive we the love of God, because he laid down his life for us: and we ought to lay down our lives for the brethren" (3:14, 16).

Peter gave the church at large this fourfold commandment: "Honour all men. Love the brotherhood. Fear God. Honour the king" (I Pet. 2:17). So important is brotherly love that Paul closed his letter to the Ephesian church, which was known for its first love, with the words, "Peace be to the brethren, and love with faith, from God the Father and the Lord Jesus Christ" (Eph. 6:23). These verses and a host of others show the extent to which the righteous should go to fulfill their responsibilities to their brothers and neighbors. Am-I-my-brother's-keeper rebels nourish and cherish themselves without acknowledging responsibility toward anyone else. The righteous live by the rule of responsibility, and they are not ashamed to show it!

3
The Poor-Me Rule

"Because I have called, and ye refused; I have stretched out my hand, and no man regarded;

"But ye have set at nought all my counsel, and would none of my reproof:

"I also will laugh at your calamity; I will mock when your fear cometh;

"When your fear cometh as desolation, and your destruction cometh as a whirlwind; when distress and anguish cometh upon you.

"Then shall they call upon me, but I will not answer; they shall seek me early, but they shall not find me:

"For that they hated knowledge, and did not choose the fear of the LORD:

"They would none of my counsel: they despised all my reproof.

"Therefore shall they eat of the fruit of their own way, and be filled with their own devices.

"For the turning away of the simple shall slay them, and the prosperity of fools shall destroy them."—Prov. 1:24–32.

Perhaps nothing is bitterer than a dosage of one's own medicine, and poor-me rebels are definitely the ones who complain the loudest when they get what is coming to them. It is trademark poor-me rebellion when the rebel complains about the taste of his just deserts. The consequences of rebellion are never pretty or enjoyable. When rebels find themselves mired in the messes brought on by their own mischief, they often start whining.

Cain

Cain demonstrated this when he told God,

> *"My punishment is greater than I can bear.*
> *"Behold, thou hast driven me out this day from the face of the earth; and from thy face shall I be hid; and I shall be a fugitive and a vagabond in the earth; and it shall come to pass, that every one that findeth me shall slay me."*—Gen. 4:13, 14.

Cain complained because of the trouble in which he had landed due to his hatred of Abel's righteousness, and he shoved his poor-me complaint into the face of God. The poor-me mentality is a psychological ploy. By employment of this tactic, the rebel can falsely comfort himself with the thought that he and his actions are somehow disconnected from the rough times that he has encountered.

Truth, on the other hand, inseparably connects sin with unpleasant consequences. Consider King David's fourfold sorrow (II Sam. 12–18), King Asa's diseased feet (II Chron. 16:12), King Belshazzar's sudden demise (Dan. 5:30) and Jezebel's gory death (II Kings 9:33).

Poor-Me Imagination

First, as a rebel, Cain first overstated his punishment, telling God outright that it was unbearable—and, by implication, unreasonable. By telling God that he could not hold up under the punishment, he was employing his rebellious imagination to ease the agony of his conscience. "The way of transgressors is hard" (Prov. 13:15), and such difficulty comes their way due to their transgressions.

The mercy of God toward Cain is obvious since Cain was

still living and was given further opportunity to bring the required offering for sin. Cain did not see that God had 'punished him less than his iniquities deserved' (Ezra 9:13). As a poor-me rebel, he imagined God's harshness and rigidness in what he deemed a punishment greater than the crime. He thus despised 'the riches of His goodness and forbearance and long-suffering; not knowing that the goodness of God was leading him to repentance; but after his hardness and impenitent heart, he treasured up unto himself wrath' (Rom. 2:4, 5).

Poor-Me Implication

Second, Cain implicated God, as if in a crime, when he complained, "Thou hast driven me out this day from the face of the earth" (Gen. 4:14). Interestingly, Cain had had no controversy with God during his lifelong *spiritual* separation from Him, but once his sin resulted in his being driven out in a *physical* manner, he was irate. This driving out from the face of the earth is explained in God's words to him: "When thou tillest the ground, it shall not henceforth yield unto thee her strength" (vs. 12). In other words, Cain would have to toil more to receive less—a brutal prospect to a man who "brought of the fruit of the ground an offering unto the LORD" (vs. 3).

When the voice of God had been soft and gentle, and when the provision of a sin offering had lain at the door, Cain worked his own way. He seemed neither to covet closeness nor wish for any blessing when things were easy and convenient and life's circumstances were pleasant. However, once the trouble came, he cursed the prospect of losing permanently so much of what he had taken for granted.

Poor-Me Irritation

In the third place, Cain cited the broken fellowship. "From thy face shall I be hid" (vs. 14) was his lament, an expression of the irritation of rebels who will not repent.

Cain did not seek or desire fellowship with God prior to that moment. However, once he was 'cursed from the earth, which had opened her mouth to receive his brother's blood' (vs. 11), he chafed under the prospect of God's hidden face. Ironically, the required sacrifice could still have been offered, and he would not have been hidden from God's face, but there is no Scripture record that Cain ever availed himself of that provision. He traveled still along his pathway of disgruntled irritation.

Poor-me rebels do not trouble themselves about their broken fellowship while they are sinning and enjoying it. The only time they pine about the loss of fellowship is at the time when the short season of sin's pleasure has ended and the bitter fruit ripens. Apart from repentance, there is no solution that will repair broken fellowship.

Poor-Me Isolation

Fourth, Cain expressed chagrin for his estrangement from men. Just as broken fellowship brought loss before God, ostracism was his lot with men. God said, "A fugitive and a vagabond shalt thou be in the earth" (vs. 12). The only other people in the world at that time were his parents and sisters, and he was being severed from them. God had not destroyed the fabric of their family joy; Cain had. Cain was personally responsible for marring the precious bond of family love that existed up to the moment he murdered his brother. Even so, he complained to God that his lot as an isolated fugitive and vagabond was too stringent.

Truly those rebels who deeply offend others generally reap by being overlooked, if not completely shunned, by those same people. Strangely, the tables turn, and the day comes when the rebel wants relationships. He then finds that, due to his poverty of spirit, his lot parallels that of the financially poor expressed in Proverbs 19:7: "All the brethren of the poor do hate him: how much more do his friends go far from him? he pursueth them with words, yet they are wanting to him."

Poor-Me Indignation

Finally, rebel Cain cried poor-me to God for exposing him to the danger of revenge. In a fit of indignation, Cain as much as told God, "You are endangering my life!" When Abel's life had been in danger, Cain seemed indifferent to peril and vulnerability; but when his own life was in danger, he became verbally agitated at God, the righteous Judge, as if God had made Cain the object of vengeance. Cain had done that to himself.

His statement that anyone who might find him would slay him is almost comical. Although slaying him would have been well within the rights of the avenger of blood, there weren't too many people who could find him. However, given that possibility, God showed clemency, setting a "mark upon Cain, lest any finding him should kill him" (Gen. 4:15). Having been shown a degree of forbearance, Cain should have responded in gratitude, but instead, he "went out from the presence of the LORD" (vs. 16) with his wife and continued on the pathway of rebellion.

The poor-me moaning of Cain and rebels like him is common. Rebels live by this rule faithfully, seeking by their sniveling to evoke the pity of those they have offended. Repentance would clear the issue every time, but Cain did not turn to God in repentance; he turned farther from God in the self-pity of poor-me rebellion.

King Saul

King Saul exhibited another side of the poor-me rule of rebellion when, in his rabid zeal against young David, he said to his servants,

"Hear now, ye Benjamites; will the son of Jesse give every

one of you fields and vineyards, and make you all captains of
thousands, and captains of hundreds;
　　"That all of you have conspired against me, and there is
none that sheweth me that my son hath made a league with
the son of Jesse, and there is none of you that is sorry for me,
or sheweth unto me that my son hath stirred up my servant
against me, to lie in wait, as at this day?"—I Sam. 22:7, 8.

In this pathetic pout of poor-me rebellion, King Saul outlined the way the poor-me rule affects relationships with people, just as Cain had manifested this rule as it plays in relation
to God.

Poor-Me Insinuation

First, the rebel king voiced a question as to whether his soldiers believed David would do for them as much as he himself
already had done. The poor-me rule often displays itself in an
inferiority complex. By asking this as a question in lieu of making an outright accusation, the king was merely insinuating
that his soldiers had had such discussions among themselves.
The poor-me rebellion of this carnal monarch entitled him
offhandedly to suspect their ingratitude and disloyalty—or so
he thought. By insinuating that they had clandestine longings
for another, better king, he actually increased the probability
that they *would* long for another king. In addition, he emphat-
ically revealed the fact of his own insecurity.

Clearly, Saul was fearful that David would take over the
kingdom. After Saul's foolish intrusion into the priest's office,
Samuel had told Saul, "The LORD hath sought him a man after
his own heart...because thou hast not kept that which the
LORD commanded thee" (I Sam. 13:14). Later, after Saul's sparing of Agag and the best sheep and oxen from the battle with
the Amalekites, Samuel prophesied to Saul, "The LORD hath
rent the kingdom of Israel from thee this day, and hath given
it to a neighbour of thine, that is better than thou" (15:28).

Once David had slain Goliath, the praises for David exceeded the praises for Saul ten times over.

King Saul had definite cause to suspect that David might well be the one of whom Samuel spoke. That fact alone became the seedbed for the inferiority mentality that plagued him (and caused him to seek David's death). Coupled with the evil spirit that troubled him, it led to an overall poor-me rebellion. But while this thought plagued Saul, his soldiers probably knew nothing of Samuel's warnings and were likely clueless as to the reasons for Saul's unpredictable outrages and self-pitying sulks.

Poor-Me Implication

In the second place, King Saul demonstrated his poor-me stance by implying that his troops would conceal state information from him in a presumed conspiracy. Poor-me rebellion also manifests itself in a *persecution complex*. His nobody-likes-me-everybody-hates-me comment was aimed at gaining the sympathies of his already hesitant and disillusioned soldiers. By launching into this childish tirade saying that none of them would side with him enough to reveal the league between his son Jonathan and young David, he was attempting to motivate his soldiers with shame rather than with wisdom and competence.

The fact is that no biblical evidence exists for such a conspiracy. Saul based this erroneous conclusion upon the fact that no one talked directly to him about the league between David and Jonathan. The soldiers felt no need to discuss this, because the covenant between David and Jonathan was public knowledge; and it was a noble, patriotic friendship. Both David and Jonathan developed goodwill and prosperity for Saul by the love they had for each other and for the kingdom. Furthermore, that no such conspiracy existed is proven once for all by the fact that, even after Saul died, it took David seven years to win the loyalty of the former followers of Saul!

Poor-Me Indiscretion

Finally, the poor-me spirit showed itself when King Saul complained that no one was sorry for him. In this, Saul's poor-me rebellion appeared as a martyrdom complex. This was an attempt to use pity to manipulate his troops into admitting where David was and what he was doing.

How silly! Where were these soldiers? They were not in the wilderness with David. The text says that "Saul abode in Gibeah under a tree in Ramah...and all his servants were standing about him" (22:6). His servants were standing within earshot, but he had the indiscretion to protest to them as though they had already defected to David! Even though King Saul yet had their loyalty and service at his command, his rebellion twisted his perception to the point where he could not even see his own men for who they were, what they were and where they were!

Whether the rebel is crying poor-me to God or man, he is attempting to manipulate others to avoid correcting himself. Rebellion is like that. It turns gallant, courageous men into whining wimps. It changes honest, holy men into childish churls. It creates moping mongrels out of men who could as easily have been holy, heroic saints.

King Ahab

In the era when Queen Jezebel sought to rid the land of Israel of the prophets of God so that prophets of Baal and the prophets of the groves could prevail, Elijah, Micaiah, Obadiah and his hundred men received unique dispensations of protection. While Jezebel manifested her audacious and fiendish lust for success, Ahab displayed poor-me rebellion throughout his reign. Because his life was also characterized by blame-the-righteous rebellion, and because the latter rule better describes Ahab, his story will receive more detailed attention in chapter 12. However, he demonstrated enough poor-me rebellion to warrant mention here as well. Elijah and Micaiah, God's two "fundamentalists," were often the audience of his poor-me moods.

First Kings 20 gives the record of Ahab's Syrian campaigns. Encouraged by the promise of victory from an unnamed prophet, the king of Israel set the battle in array and was victorious. The prophet came back and warned Ahab to regroup and strengthen his forces because the Syrians would attack again. Foolishly thinking that God was God only of the hills, the superstitious Syrians planned an attack in the plains. Again, the unnamed man of God assured Ahab of triumph to prove to Ahab that God is the Lord.

In a miraculous outpouring of God's power, the greatly outnumbered Israelite army routed the Syrians, but Ahab foolishly spared Benhadad, king of Syria, invoking the Lord's anger. Ahab was told by God's man that his life would go for Benhadad's, an announcement that sent Ahab into a downward spiral of sullenness.

Poor-Me Invalidation

The next chapter tells of Ahab's atrocious travesty against Naboth of Jezreel, an honest citizen and God-fearing subject. Having coveted Naboth's vineyard and discovering that Naboth would not sell or trade, the king descended even further into poor-me moping of colossal proportions. His wife, Jezebel, orchestrated a lie-filled mock trial; Naboth was stoned, and Ahab took the vineyard.

Upon Ahab's arrival there to inspect the vineyard, Elijah met him. Ahab's first words were a poor-me invalidation if ever there was one: "Hast thou found me, O mine enemy?" (I Kings 21:20). Angered that he could not so much as have one afternoon to cheer up himself without having Elijah show up to "spoil the party," he resorted to invalidating God's prophet. For Ahab to attribute the word *enemy* to Elijah when he himself was the real enemy of righteousness and goodness was a treacherous invalidation of one whose resume included the *authority* and *approbation* and *audience* of God.

After three years, Ahab determined to recapture the city of Ramoth-Gilead from Syria. Enlisting the help of Jehoshaphat of Judah, Ahab gathered together his four hundred prophets (22:6) to ask counsel. Their foolish, demonic counsel was that Ahab would go out and return with the city in his possession and the spoils to boot. Jehoshaphat asked, "Is there not here a prophet of the LORD besides, that we might enquire of him?" (vs. 7). Ahab again sported his poor-me invalidation attitude: "There is yet one man, Micaiah the son of Imlah, by whom we may enquire of the LORD: but I hate him; for he doth not prophesy good concerning me, but evil" (vs. 8).

Here is King Ahab, rebellious from the first mention to the last, seeking to invalidate the credentials of a holy man of God. Ahab rebelled by walking in the sins of Jeroboam, the son of Nebat, who made Israel to sin. He rebelled by marrying Jezebel, daughter of Ethbaal, a Zidonian (not a Jew). He rebelled by worshiping Baal and rearing up groves to that abomination. He rebelled by rejecting the prophecy of Joshua concerning the rebuilding of Jericho. He rebelled against the prophecy of Elijah and sought with his wife to have Elijah killed after the revival on Mt. Carmel. He rebelled in sparing Benhadad when God had told him to destroy this Syrian king. He rebelled in joining with his evil wife in the unnecessary and unlawful death of Naboth. He rebelled by listening to the lying prophets one too many times.

After all that rebellion, he dared to invalidate the prophet Micaiah with his poor-me self-pity! He dared to cry foul when Micaiah had nothing good to say about him: "But...he doth not prophesy good concerning me, but evil." The poor-me stench of his comments permeates the passage! Ahab plied the trade of poor-me rebellion as if he could alleviate his guilt and perhaps mitigate the promised judgment of God! He longed for the soft feelings of others even when his heart was hard and calloused toward them.

Rebels who are boxed in and facing a pending doom will often resort to the poor-me rule. It is one more of many rules they live by so they can avoid repentance and stay in love with their sins.

Illustration

A church member whose faithfulness was evident came to his pastor one evening after the service. The man's son was developing a poor-me rebellion. Regardless of what means the father and mother attempted to employ to correct his errant behavior, their son convinced himself that his parents and siblings were all ganging up against him. The pastor called the son into the conversation, and immediately he cried out to his father, "Don't you have enough people on your side? Do you have to turn the pastor against me too?" Not three weeks later, this young man was caught red-handed in a class A felony. Because there were three living witnesses whose testimonies were corroborated by videotape, the son was sentenced to stiff fines and a lengthy jail term. The father later testified that whenever he would visit his son in the prison, the conversation always eventually turned to poor-me and why-me attitudes. Tried, found guilty and convicted, he still maintained that everyone was against him.

The Rule That the Righteous Live By

Endurance

Hebrews 12 gives the classic Scripture on chastening. The

way out of poor-me rebellion is the endurance of the chastening that comes. It is this response to chastening that delivers poor-me rebels and turns them into righteous believers.

First, the righteous do not despise the chastening of the Lord; rather, they come to appreciate it. This involves fully embracing the concept that chastening is one of the strongest evidences of God's love (not of His disgust). The righteous do not faint under God's rebuke.

Second, once the righteous become appreciative, they subject themselves to change, purposing to have a reverent and eager willingness to abandon the behavior that brought the chastening so they can begin to partake of His holiness. Poor-me rebels continue in the antics that brought on the chastening; the righteous put off those old-nature ways and put on new-nature ways.

Third, the righteous believer works for a different harvest. Chastening "yieldeth the peaceable fruit of righteousness unto them which are exercised thereby" (vs. 11). This exercising is literally a callisthenic, a routine of discipline such as what one would practice for Olympic games. Such daily training transforms ordinary people into excellent athletes, and in the spiritual application of this passage, poor-me rebels who allow God's chastening to train them can eventually produce righteousness.

Fourth, and finally, the righteous believer must lift up his drooping hands and follow on in the pathway of God's design, this time "looking diligently lest [he] fail of the grace of God" (vs. 15); that is, lest he falter in the appropriation of God's restorative purposes. The warning about Esau in the passage applies to the poor-me rebel who does not repent but simply has remorse and becomes embittered when his falsity does not merit him the blessing.

The righteous believer who is duly exercised by the chastening of the Lord and sees the peaceable fruit of righteousness begin to ripen is in position for Romans 8:28 to become a reality. The poor-me rebel can never enter the rooms of blessing and the recesses of sweetness afforded in that verse. However, once a poor-me rebel has endured and been straightened out by the chastening hand of God, the joys of that verse can become real. The promise that "all things work together for good" is predicated upon two conditions: one, that the person love God, and two, that the person be called according to God's purpose. It is obvious that a poor-me rebel meets neither condition.

But once a poor-me rebel has endured chastening and has learned from it, he can come back to loving God and can enter (or re-enter) the calling of God. From that moment on, he will not be a poor-me rebel, whining about all the trouble God brings. He will be a bless-my-soul, righteous believer who rejoices in all the wonderful ways that God works despite all the Devil's efforts to frustrate and thwart!

4
The Compromise-to-Gain-Good Rule

"Correction is grievous unto him that forsaketh the way: and he that hateth reproof shall die."

"The fear of the LORD tendeth to life: and he that hath it shall abide satisfied; he shall not be visited with evil."—Prov. 15:10; 19:23.

"Why trimmest thou thy way to seek love? therefore hast thou also taught the wicked ones thy ways."—Jer. 2:33.

"For what is a man advantaged, if he gain the whole world, and lose himself, or be cast away?"—Luke 9:25.

A rebel regularly lives by the rule of compromise in any given situation if it is thought that such evil will effect later good for himself. The primary evil in which this type of rebel engages is the abandonment of right principle for the presumed advantage of future opportunity. This rule makes evildoing acceptable—even approvable—if the rebel perceives that the evil will lead to a personal advantage. Such pragmatic faith that the end justifies the means forgets that the means determine the end.

Lot

Lot's early life is obscure except for the fact that, as Abraham's nephew, he was well-acquainted with a man of faith.

After Lot settled in the land of promise and became wealthier, a strife between his herdsmen and the herdsmen of Abraham led to their separating from each other. Abraham asked a telling question: "Is not the whole land before thee?" (Gen. 13:9). Lot could have gone anywhere, but he went to the wrong place. Lot did a good thing to give space to his uncle, but he compromised by moving into the proximity of, and subsequently the fellowship of, people whom he well knew "were wicked and sinners before the LORD exceedingly" (vs. 13).

Bible commentators differ in their analysis of Lot's evildoing. Regardless of any man's assessments, God referred to "just Lot...that righteous man," classifying him as one justified by faith. God also related that Lot was "vexed with the filthy conversation of the wicked" because by "dwelling among them, in seeing and hearing, [he] vexed his righteous soul from day to day with their unlawful deeds" (II Pet. 2:7, 8). Plainly, Lot compromised for the gain he thought he could reap from it. His vexation of soul was the result, as it always is, of a *tolerance* of evil that led to a *practice* of evil.

Compromise-to-Gain-Good Desire

Lot's rebellion of compromise to gain good first showed in his desire. When he "lifted up his eyes, and beheld all the plain of Jordan, that it was well watered every where...even as the garden of the LORD" (Gen. 13:10), he was demonstrating an inner lust for the good things of this world rather than an inner striving for the good things of the next. Instead of honing spiritual desires that would have led him anywhere but to Sodom, he had cultivated carnal desires, and those carnal impulses had come to possess him. His reasoning was probably, "What's wrong with green trees and irrigated property? I can grow more than I need and help others." He cited the potential good he could do while ignoring the principle he was violating. He compromised.

Compromise-to-Gain-Good Decision

Lot continued to rebel in compromising to gain good in his decision. "Lot chose him all the plain of Jordan" (vs. 11), knowing full well the spiritual bankruptcy and moral debauchery of that place. His association with the sodomites who "were wicked and sinners before the LORD exceedingly" (vs. 13) was not a happenstance or unfortunate development. Having already lived in that area for some time with his godly Uncle Abraham, Lot well knew the moral and spiritual status of that abominable place. Like neoevangelicals of the past six millennia, he rationalized away the evil of his decision by visualizing unborn good and untapped expediency that the future would afford him.

Compromise-to-Gain-Good Direction

The third way Lot was a compromising rebel showed up in his direction. Verse 11 states simply, "Lot journeyed east"; that is, in the direction of sin. That is not to say that sin is always eastward, or that the eastward direction is sinful. For Lot, however, east was the wrong direction! He went toward the most evil and corrupt society on record for that era in history. His direction openly manifested his rebellion, not only against God but also against Abraham who most certainly must have offered both warning and advice against such a move.

To move in a direction that is away from godly people is dangerous. Of course, Lot and Abraham had to separate geographically and physically so that the herds and flocks would have sufficient grazing acreage. It is not this separation that is evil. It is the separation from the man Abraham that was evil. It is the separation unto Sodom that was evil. Lot walked aloof from godliness when he journeyed. He wandered far from righteousness in that journey eastward, and he never returned. While doing a good thing in giving his uncle space, he did an evil thing in the space he elected to occupy.

Compromise-to-Gain-Good Dwelling

Once Lot had directed his life toward Sodom, he manifested the compromise-to-gain-good rule of rebellion by his
dwelling: "Lot dwelled in the cities of the plain, and pitched his
tent toward Sodom" (vs. 12). This is not a case of a rebel who
had a month-long stint exploring the world and, finding it
repugnant, repented and, in humility, went back to God. To
the contrary, he settled down in the midst of evil. Scripture
says he dwelled in the cities (not "city"—singular), which
might indicate a restlessness and a moving from place to place
among the sodomites. Of course, there is no peace or rest to
the wicked, and his inability to find satisfaction would picture
any believer's futile quest for true fulfillment in this world.
Were he to have awakened to the emptiness of his pursuits, he
might well have returned to Abraham and Abraham's God.
Instead, he continued pell-mell along the path of compromising to gain good. He just knew his opportunity to gain good
was just around the next bend. Had one asked Lot about his
behavior, he would likely have responded that he had not done
anything that could be classified as specifically disobedient to
a direct command.

Genesis 14 records some historical facts about Gentile
powers who had formed two opposing factions. There was a
battle between an alliance of four kings against an alliance of
five. Due to his dwelling in sodomite territory, Lot was captured in this combat; and Abraham, joined by three Amorite
brothers who were his confederates, went with his household of over three hundred and delivered Lot.

Compromise-to-Gain-Good Denial

In the fifth place, Lot showed his rebellion of compromising to gain good in his denial. At the end of the battle,

Melchizedek, the priest of the most high God, and the king of Sodom met with Abraham. It is highly likely that Lot was also in that company. He had just witnessed the miraculous deliverance of God when a few hundred of Abraham's men and their friends miraculously overcame several kings. He then witnessed Abraham's words to Melchizedek and Sodom's king, and he denied God in the presence of them all and walked away back to Sodom and sin. He was still reasoning that he could gain good in Sodom, and he was compromising to gain it.

Compromise-to-Gain-Good Delusion

For the next four chapters, Genesis is silent about Lot. His story picks up again in chapter 19 where his sixth evidence of compromise-to-gain-good rebellion is announced: "Lot sat in the gate of Sodom" (vs. 1). Here, Lot's delusion is portrayed. Like the compromisers of every age, he was deluded into attempting to gain good by getting into an advisory position among the enemies. His sitting in that gate was a pivotal event in the evil of his life. God has never called any man to 'sit in the seat of the scornful' (Ps. 1:1); in fact, God has commanded the opposite.

Compromise-to-Gain-Good Destruction

Seventh, and finally, Lot's compromise-to-gain-good rebellion led to his destruction. The destruction Lot experienced was threefold. His efforts to gain good by doing evil led to the destruction of his *inheritance*; his warning to his sons-in-law of pending doom upon the cities of the plain was rejected with sarcastic ridicule. The seat of influence he had attained by compromise was snatched away in a night. Next, he saw the destruction of the *inhabitants* of the cities where he had so long ago determined to do so much good. Sadly, this portion of the destruction included the turning of his wife into a pillar of salt. Finally, he experienced the destruction of his *inhibitions* as his biblical biography ends with him living as a fearful, cave-dwelling vagabond in drunken incest with his own daughters!

The Tribes of Reuben and Gad and the Half-Tribe of Manasseh

Just as Lot pictures the compromise-to-gain-good rule of rebellion in an individual, the two and one-half tribes that chose to remain outside the Promised Land after Joshua's conquest of Canaan demonstrate it as it applies to groups. Every organized grouping of rebels with leaders and followers can be shown to operate by the exact rules that the rebels themselves observe individually. This is specifically applicable to the tribes who rebelliously selected the land "on this side Jordan near Jericho eastward, toward the sunrising" (Num. 34:15). God had promised and provided them a different land; they chose their own.

The biblical record of the settlement of Canaan in Deuteronomy and Joshua shows that the lands of Seir, Moab and Ammon were *prohibited lands.* God told Moses, "Meddle not with them; for I will not give you of their land...Distress [them] not...neither contend with them in battle" (Deut. 2:5, 9, 19). Of course, there was also the *Promised Land* that has been apportioned to the descendants of Abraham ever since God made his covenant with Abraham in Genesis. The land of promise was God's unique and specific provision for the children of Israel; it was His gift to them. Israel was to *purge* that territory of its wicked occupants, *possess* that territory as its own and *prosper* in that territory under the blessing which God would place upon them within the protective boundaries He had prescribed.

Somewhat less noticeable but equally a part of the division of the land is the *purchased lands* of Sihon, the Amorite king of

Heshbon, and Og, king of Bashan, that became the *permitted lands* of Reuben, Gad and one-half of Manasseh. These two kings and their people were routed by Israel in the final days of their approach to Canaan (Num. 21:21–35) just prior to the curse of Balaam and the numbering of the new generation. God allowed Moses to lead the Israelites in massive, decisive victories over Sihon and Og. Their lands were purchased by the military effort of God's people.

After the entire nation had conquered these lands, the tribes of Reuben and Gad and the half tribe of Manasseh approached Moses and said,

> "The country which the LORD smote...is a land for cattle, and thy servants have cattle:
>
> "Wherefore...if we have found grace in thy sight, let this land be given unto thy servants for a possession, and bring us not over Jordan"—Num. 32:4, 5.

In other words, these two and one-half tribes were compromising the command and promise of God for the good they could gain by having prime grazing land for their cattle. Incidentally, God's promise to Israel in the land included His provision for adequate crops and healthy animals (Exod. 23:26; Lev. 26:4, 5), so the supposed need for this grazing land was either negligently ignorant or purely carnal.

Regardless, Moses' immediate confrontation of their rebellion was met with the assurance of the two and one-half tribes that Moses had nothing to be concerned about, that they would "go ready armed before the children of Israel, until we have brought them unto their place" (Num. 32:17) prior to returning to those lands purchased by their military conquest. These purchased lands were to become permitted lands as Moses, in fashion similar to Samuel's later dealings with Israel when they demanded a king, gave in to their insistence. Rebels will rebel, whether one protests or permits. "If a wise man contendeth with a foolish man, whether he rage or laugh, there is no rest" (Prov. 29:9).

It is not until Joshua 22 that the fullness of this rebellion is recorded in Scripture. By that time, Israel had sufficiently possessed the land that they could dwell there and divide it among the tribes. They had been shown the borders God had provided for each tribe individually and for the nation collectively.

When "Joshua called the Reubenites, and the Gadites, and the half tribe of Manasseh" (vs. 1), it was to commend them for having assisted their brethren from the other tribes in the conquest of the Promised Land and to permit them to cross back to the eastern side of Jordan to inhabit the lands they had chosen. Even then, he made in this chapter the final offer that "if the land of your possession be unclean, then pass ye over unto the land of the possession of the LORD, wherein the LORD's tabernacle dwelleth, and take possession among us" (vs.. 19). With this background established, a full examination of the compromise-to-gain-good rule among groups is now possible.

Compromise-to-Gain-Good Possession

Groups display the compromise-to-gain-good rule in the matter of possession. One must note in Joshua's statement in verse 19 the contrast between "your possession" and "the possession of the Lord." There are many references to the nine and one-half tribes possessing the Promised Land. It is spiritually enlightening to contrast these to this statement of Joshua and the one in verse 9 concerning the two and one-half tribes: "And the children of Reuben and the children of Gad and the half tribe of Manasseh returned, and departed from the children of Israel out of Shiloh…to go unto the country of Gilead, to *the land of their possession, whereof they were possessed.*" (emphasis mine).

This verse reads like an Old Testament version of I John

2:19: "They went out from us, but they were not of us; for if they had been of us, they would no doubt have continued with us: but they went out, that they might be made manifest that they were not all of us." Rebels never have part and lot with the spiritual heirs of the promises of God. Spiritual people possess their possessions; rebels are possessed by their possessions. Spiritual people are masters of what they possess; rebels becomes mastered by what they possess.

Compromise-to-Gain-Good Priority

The next characteristic of compromising to gain good among groups is their priority. God had authorized Joshua to rear up a heap of twelve stones that men had lifted out of the Jordan River and piled up on the western shore of Jordan to commemorate the miraculous dry-land crossing into the Promised Land (Josh. 4:19–24). The purpose of this heap of stones included the fact that future generations could ask for its meaning. They could then be told about God's wonderful work of drying up the Jordan just like He had dried up the Red Sea so that children and children's children could know the might and power of the hand of the Lord. This heap of twelve stones could not have been very large, because a man cannot lift up a very large stone. Perhaps this heap of twelve stones was six feet high.

The priority of this monument was not visibility, but commemoration. God did not want that heap of stones to be an enormous mound, visible from the distance. He desired it to be small in size so that in order to find it, people would need to seek it and come close to it. This is much like it is with God. He who would find God must seek Him and draw near to Him.

In stark contrast, the "great altar to see to" was called just that because its priority was visibility (22:10). Compromisers frequently place themselves within the visibility and vicinity of the godly in order to appear godly to uninformed onlookers. This is what Reuben, Gad and Manasseh hoped to achieve.

When people came to celebrate the dry-land crossing and teach their children about God's wonders, those same curious children would say, "Daddy, what is that big altar on the other side of the river? It looks interesting. Can we go see it? Why not, Daddy? What can be so wrong with it?" Reuben, Gad and Manasseh could have erected their altar anywhere in the land of Gilead or Bashan, but the rebels placed it where it could have the greatest drawing power and influence. Those who compromise to gain good prioritize "to be seen of men" (Matt. 23:5) and enjoy placing themselves in prime visibility where their compromise can effect the most influential appearance of success.

Incidentally, there is no record of Jordan drying up before Reuben, Gad and Manasseh as they carnally returned to their permitted lands. God does not perform miracles for compromise-to-gain-good rebels; rather, He turns their *walking* into *wading*. It is always harder to *wade in compromise* than to *walk in conformity* to God.

Compromise-to-Gain-Good Problems

Another way the group concept of compromise-to-gain-good rebellion shows is in the problems it creates. Truthfully, everyone has problems, and compromisers will often cite this fact when confronted with their problems. The difference is plain to any discerning eye. Problems that come because you are walking with the Lord are caused by others; rebellious compromisers cause their own problems.

The immediate result of this "great altar to see to" was *division* within the nation (Josh. 22:12–14), *confusion* about its purpose (vss. 15, 16), *erosion* of separation (vss. 17, 18) and *occasion* for judgment (vss. 19, 20). The problems that beset the righteous and godly do not bring division, confusion, erosion and occasion for judgment; rather, they bring about the good fruits of the Father's pruning and purging. Compromise always brings divisive, destructive problems whether it is an individual or a group that is compromising. The good that Reuben, Gad and the half-tribe of Manasseh gained in having prime grazing land for their cows and sheep and goats came at the immediate cost of serious problems.

Compromise-to-Gain-Good Pacification

Whenever problems arise, those who compromise to gain good show themselves in the way they attempt to solve them: pacifism. God's instruction to the godly is always separation and purification; compromisers always resort to pacification and toleration. As the leaders of the two and one-half compromising tribes responded to Joshua and Eleazar, they sounded *spiritual* (vss. 21–23, 29), they sounded *logical* (vss. 24, 25) and they sounded *natural* (vss. 26–28).

Note for your own record that they merely *sounded* spiritual, logical and natural. The substance of what these compromisers said was unspiritual, illogical and unnatural. They were unspiritual in their vain repetitions of the name of God, in their invoking of falsely motivated punishments upon themselves *if* they were really wrong, and in the bold folly of saying "God forbid that we should rebel against the LORD" when they had already done so! The whole altar was in direct rebellion against the Lord, not only in its materials but in its overall purpose.

These compromising tribes were illogical in hypothetically imagining that the tribes in the land would say that Jordan was the border (Hadn't God said it was?) and use that as a point of separation from those tribes outside the land. Compromisers want to live outside what God provides and requires, yet they practice illogical criticism of spiritual people who classify them as "outside." If a person is outside, it is the epitome of illogical folly to say he is inside!

Finally, these tribes were unnatural in stating that this altar was simply for a witness. God *never* commanded His people to erect an altar as a witness. Altars were for sacrifice, and the fact that the compromising tribes explained this as an altar of witness showed their desire to pacify.

Compromise-to-Gain-Good Product

The product of the compromise-to-gain-good rebellion in Joshua 22 was tragic. The immediate, later and ultimate results of that compromise brought agony to everyone involved.

One of the *immediate results* of that compromise is seen in the distribution of the cities of refuge. Joshua 20:7, 8 list Kedesh, Shechem and Kirjath-arba as the three cities of refuge in the Promised Land west of Jordan, and Bezer, Ramoth and Golan as cities of refuge in the permitted land on the eastern side of the Jordan River where the compromisers settled.

Cities of refuge were given for safety to any person involved in the accidental death of another person. This could indicate that God's protection was more powerful on the west side of Jordan in the Promised Land than upon the east side in the permitted land, because two and one-half tribes on the east side needed as many cities of refuge as nine and one-half tribes required on the west side.

God protects where He provides, but His divine protection lessens when a person compromises and gets out of the way that God *provides* and into the way that God *permits*. The fact that twenty percent of the population needed as many cities of refuge as the other eighty percent indicates that those who obeyed were one-fourth as likely to be involved in accidental deaths as those who compromised.

Another immediate result of the compromise-to-gain-good

rebellion was that among the priests, princes and people, no one had enough spiritual understanding and backbone to discern and confront the compromise. The compromise was contrived in such clever means and defended in such artful terms that Phinehas the priest said, "This day we perceive that the LORD is among us, because ye have not committed this trespass against the LORD" (22:31). The response of Phinehas "pleased the children of Israel; and the children of Israel blessed God, and did not intend to go up against them in battle" (vs. 33). The compromise had infected the entire nation, and they were pleased to appease the compromise rather than eliminate it. The whole nation said "amen" and went on as if no compromise had occurred.

The *later results* of that compromise as it infiltrated the land were visible in the ongoing cycles of apostasy and bondage and judgment in the period of the judges which ensued after the deaths of Joshua and Eleazar. Israel compromised with the wicked nations that God had told them to utterly obliterate. Rather than destroy those idolatrous, perverted people, Israel compromised to gain the good of their servitude. They did not drive out those peoples (Judg.1:21, 27-33) but cohabited with them and made them tributaries and servants. In Judges 3:5, it says they were living among six of the seven nations they were told to destroy (Deut. 7:1).

The natural outcome of this compromise-to-gain-good rebellion was that "they took their daughters to be their wives, and gave their daughters to their sons, and served their gods" (Judg. 3:6). Had Joshua and Eleazar and Phinehas and the princes of Israel stood up to Reuben, Gad and the half-tribe of Manasseh and said, "Tear down your altar, or we'll tear it down," it is possible that the entire nation would have also stood up to the greater threats of the heathen among them. As is the pattern, compromise-to-gain-good rebellion tolerates increasing levels of sin until no distinction can be discerned at all between the rebel and the righteous.

The *ultimate results* of that compromise-to-gain-good rebellion are found much later in God's Word. The record of King Solomon's officers lists a son of Geber to whom "pertained the towns of Jair...which are in Gilead; to him also pertained the region of Argob, which is in Bashan" (I Kings 4:13). Later in this roster, the Spirit of God mentioned Geber himself who "was in the country of Gilead, in the country of Sihon king of the Amorites, and of Og king of Bashan; and he was the only officer which was in the land" (vs. 19). Besides Ahinadab, who was in Mahanaim, this man Geber and his son were the only ones mentioned as having leadership in the land on the east of Jordan, and Geber was the only actual officer. It was as if generations of compromise had rendered Reuben, Gad and the half-tribe of Manasseh a careless people, disinterested in and intolerant of government. Such lax oversight on Solomon's part allowed that region, formerly under the idolatrous kings Sihon and Og, to descend into a bastion of compromise and a breeding ground for apostasy.

Verses 20–25 speak of Judah and Israel "eating and drinking, and making merry" and dwelling "safely, every man under his vine and under his fig tree." Solomon's dominion included the enormous land mass extending northeast all the way to Tiphsah on the Euphrates and southwest all the way to the river of Egypt. Perhaps having so gigantic a kingdom rendered him disinterested in fortifying or managing the property on the east side of Jordan. Maybe the apparent submission so common to compromising people deceived Solomon into believing that Reuben, Gad and the half-tribe of Manasseh did not need strong and decisive leadership. Possibly, Solomon had a subtle identification with those compromising tribes because he himself was on the verge of his own personal compromises. Whatever the reason, history records that he did not oblige himself to stem the tide of compromises practiced in the region previously held by Sihon and Og.

First Chronicles 5:8, 9 records the interesting tidbit that Bela, one of Reuben's descendents, went still further eastward and "inhabited unto the entering in of the wilderness from the river Euphrates: because their cattle were multiplied in the land of Gilead." This compromise-to-gain-good rule was being lived out by Reuben's descendents generations later. They were still moving eastward—not westward toward God's Promised Land—and they were still making their compromising choices based on the good of grazing room for their cattle!

Second Kings 10:32, 33 records the conquest of Reuben, Gad and Manasseh in the permitted land of Gilead and Bashan. They were more vulnerable to Syrian attack than the other tribes because they did not have the Jordan River as a defensive barrier. The decision of their ancestors to settle there was still bearing fruit. The bottom line is that when rebels compromise to gain good, they actually remove themselves and their descendants from the blessing and protection of God. They end up tolerant of all manner of sin, unmanaged and unmanageable in lifestyle, entrenched in traditions of compromise, vulnerable to attack, powerless in the battle and defeated long before their spiritual counterparts.

Illustration

Consider the preacher who discovered that his treasurer was dipping into the church offerings. When he spoke to the treasurer, the treasurer said, "Preacher, I know it's not the best practice, but I need some extra cash for a family vacation. I was planning to do this for only a few weeks until I could gather enough for a few extra days off." One could easily argue that a family vacation is a good thing, as are family togetherness and relaxation; however, it cannot be agreed that it is proper practice for a church treasurer to compromise the trust that others have vested in him. The compromise to gain good, in this case, was scandalously evil and, had not the pastor intervened, would have most surely led to greater compromises and further pilfering for other "good" projects.

The Rule That the Righteous Live By

Completion (Balance)

The rule the righteous live by is completion. The word "complete" in Colossians 2:10 and 4:12 comes from a root word that means "full, leveled up (as a hollow in the earth), satisfied (as a tray in a balance)." The proper philosophy of righteous Christian living involves *being* complete in Christ in salvation and *standing* complete in Christ in sanctification.

Compromise and completion are both in the middle, but they are not in the same middle. Compromise is a middle achieved when parties involved *give* something valuable away; completion (i.e., balance) is a middle achieved when individuals or parties *receive* something valuable.

Marriage illustrates this quite well. Counselors who advise husbands and wives to compromise are actually defrauding both. On the other hand, those who would counsel both husband and wife to receive all the good the other has to offer would enrich both. Interestingly, the term "help meet" from Genesis 2:20 (two words, not one) means "a help who surrounds or completes." There is not to be compromise in marriage, but completion. Since marriage illustrates Christ and his church, it follows that compromise is just as damaging to Christian living as it is to marriage; God's design is completion.

First, the righteous believer is complete in Christ, "which is the head of all principality and power: In whom also ye are circumcised with the circumcision made without hands, in putting off the body of the sins of the flesh by the circumcision of Christ" (Col. 2:10, 11). Investigation of these verses and those that follow, where the Holy Ghost speaks of being "risen with him through the faith of the operation of God" and being "quickened together with him" and being "forgiven...all trespasses," makes the passage a salvation passage.

The one who was a sinner is complete in his sainthood in the salvation he has in Christ. In that salvation, there is room for no one else, because Christ has fully paid the debt. The former sinner, now a saint, is leveled up, as it were, where he once was hollow and empty. His sin debt is fully satisfied. There is no lack, no deficit, no minus to his salvation whereby he will one day find himself sold short and missing Heaven. In Christ, he is completely saved.

Second, the righteous believer is complete in Christ when he "stand[s] perfect and complete in all the will of God" (4:12). Here, the completion is that which a believer can find when he is sanctified unto the holy will of God for his life. The one who does his own will is empty, not full. He is crammed with worldliness and carnality, not with Christ. He is hollow and unfulfilled, not leveled up in the way and work of Christ. He is dissatisfied, never fully joyful, never finding life but always losing it. How stark is the contrast when one stands in the will of God! He is full to the brim with the purpose and joy of the Lord. His life is filled up, not to be emptied by the emptiers of this world. His whole being is satisfied, because he has "apprehend[ed] that for which also [he was] apprehended of Christ Jesus" (Phil. 3:12).

The compromise-to-gain-good rebel may never be saved. He may actually think that God will compromise with him so they can meet in the middle somewhere on the matters of forgiveness, redemption, reconciliation, etc. If the compromise-to-gain-good rebel is a believer—albeit a shallow one—he will attempt all the way along to compromise with God so they can meet in the middle in matters of life calling, life work and life fruit. The compromise-to-gain-good rebel can never "lay hold on eternal life, whereunto [he is] also called" (I Tim. 6:12).

The righteous, however, are complete, having "all things that pertain unto life and godliness, through the knowledge of him that hath called [them] to glory and virtue" (II Pet. 1:3). These lack nothing they need. They confess, "O LORD, are not thine eyes upon the truth" (Jer. 5:3), and they fully grasp that truth for their lives.

If Lot had done the will of God, he would probably have merited mention in Hebrews 11, and the outcome of his life would have been diametrically opposite of what it was. If the tribes of Reuben, Gad and Manasseh had done the will of God, their posterity could have enjoyed much more of the promise of God.

Let it be announced, once and for all, that compromise-to-gain-good rebels are never complete in all the will of God; rather, they live their lives incomplete and yearning. The righteous live by the rule of completion in Christ, and they find rest.

5
The Defy-Your-Parents Rule

"He that wasteth his father, and chaseth away his mother, is a son that causeth shame, and bringeth reproach."—Prov. 19:26.

"For the son dishonoureth the father, the daughter riseth up against her mother, the daughter in law against her mother in law; a man's enemies are the men of his own house."—Mic. 7:6.

"Backbiters, haters of God, despiteful, proud, boasters, inventors of evil things, disobedient to parents."—Rom. 1:30.

"For men shall be lovers of their own selves, covetous, boasters, proud, blasphemers, disobedient to parents, unthankful, unholy."—II Tim. 3:2.

The Romans text cited above appears in a passage detailing that downward-spiraling process of mankind in his responses to God as time and mankind together are "hasting unto the coming of the day of God" (II Pet. 3:12). The verse from II Timothy is a citation of a "last days" condition that has befallen world cultures prior to the second coming of Christ. In both it and the Romans text, the phrase "disobedient to parents" occurs; therefore, the category of rebellion to which this chapter is devoted is an ongoing, sin-nature phenomenon. This rule that rebels live by is as old as mankind itself.

Ishmael

There are few parents in Scripture of whom God makes much commentary; therefore, Abraham is exceptional in that God says of him, "For I know him, that he will command his children and his household after him, and they shall keep the way of the LORD, to do justice and judgment; that the LORD may bring upon Abraham that which he hath spoken of him" (Gen. 18:19). Despite God's commendation of Abraham as a father, Ishmael rebelled in the defy-your-parents way. While Scripture depicts several defy-your-parents rebels, Ishmael is a prominent example whose biblical biography offers informative details of this rule that rebels live by.

Defy-Your-Parents Determination

The first revelation that God made about Ishmael after naming him is that God told Hagar, "He will be a wild man" (16:12). When the Lord makes a prophecy regarding what a person will be like, He is not limiting or forcing or predestining that person to conform to that mold. Instead, God is simply employing His foreknowledge, His ability to know the end from the beginning and outline what that person will determine to be in his earthly lifetime. In this statement, the Lord was informing Hagar ahead of time what her son's chief characteristic would be.

It is essential to recognize that God said, "He *will* be a wild man"; God did not say, "He will *have to* be a wild man." Ishmael was going to be a wild man by *personal determination,* not by *predestinated dictation.* Ishmael was not coerced into mocking Isaac on the day of Isaac's weaning, nor was he required by some inner clock to be a wild man. Ishmael had identical opportunity with Isaac to become a man of faith. Through the exercise of his sinful will, he brutishly rejected the wooing of Jehovah God and embraced the enticements of his flesh and of the world around him. He determined to become wild, but he did not have to be wild.

The term "wild man" is the first usage of the word "wild" in Scripture. This word means "running an undisciplined, uncharted course" in the sense of having no restraint or boundary. It is used primarily in references to wild beasts and specifically referring to the wild donkey, an animal widely reputed to be entirely abandoned to stubborn, untamed ways.

This word *wild* is also used in II Kings 4:38–40 (wild vine) to describe the unknown, uncultivated gourds that the sons of the prophets shredded into the pottage that subsequently poisoned those who ate it. Furthermore, this word is used in Isaiah 5:1–4 in the phrase "wild grapes" where Isaiah likened Israel's uncircumcised heart to uncultivated fruits in stark contrast to the good grapes that God expected to reap from His "choicest vine."

The "wild man"—the defy-your-parents rebel—is first defiant to God. Despite the best efforts of Abraham—or any other father for that matter—this type of rebel reacts negatively to authority because he is symbolically shaking his fist in the face of God. Ishmael, whose very name means "God hears," made such choices that God heard his defiance, not his worship. When Ishmael was thirteen years of age, Jehovah appeared to his parents to change his father's name from Abram ("high father") to Abraham ("father of many nations") and to change his mother's name from Sarai ("dominant one") to Sarah ("princess"). It is not written, but it is certainly sensible to expect that Abraham and Sarah took this opportunity to explain to Ishmael once again the meaning of his name and to encourage him to draw near to the God who hears those who call upon Him. Such an encouragement to draw nearer to God fell upon Ishmael's parent-defying, rebellious ears, and he drew *away* from God, not *toward* Him.

Ishmael, the defy-your-parents rebel of Genesis, fits all

three connotations that Scripture uses of the word "wild." First, like the "wild ass used to the wilderness, that snuffeth up the wind at her pleasure" (Jer. 2:24), Ishmael demonstrated unruly, rebellious lack of restraint through his hasty carelessness with important spiritual matters. Possessing a name that would ever remind him of his Creator and Lord, he ignored the value of that Creator-God and neglected to speak humbly to the God who hears. Circumcised in flesh, he never entertained the spiritual meaning of that event, never submitted to circumcision of the heart and, therefore, failed to enter into the blessing of it. Bypassed as the chief heir, he never valued the favor of either Abraham or Isaac and instead mocked and ridiculed his way into being cast out for good.

In the same way that the wild gourds were unknown to the sons of the prophets until the eaters became ill, the degree of poison in Ishmael's rebellion was hidden from Abraham until Sarah finally urged him to "cast out the bondwoman and her son" (Gal. 4:30). But that poison did not stop there, nor did the sons of men cease then to die from that poison. In the next generation, there would be another pair of sons, Esau and Jacob, and their story would be a reflection of the story of Ishmael and Isaac, with one being a man of flesh and the other a man of faith.

Interestingly, but not surprisingly, when it came time for Esau, the fleshly one of the two, to marry,

"Esau...took to wife Judith the daughter of Beeri the Hittite, and Bashemath the daughter of Elon the Hittite:

"Which were a grief of mind unto Isaac and to Rebekah"— Gen. 26:34, 35.

The story continues,

"And Esau seeing that the daughters of Canaan pleased not Isaac his father;

"Then went Esau to Ishmael, and took unto the wives

which he had Mahalath the daughter of Ishmael Abraham's son, the sister of Nebajoth, to be his wife"—28:8, 9.

Thus Ishmael ensured that his evil influence would be transferred to the next generation.

Again, as God looked for Israel to bring forth rich, juicy grapes, so Abraham looked for Ishmael to bring forth living fruit in measure with his opportunity. Ishmael was as much a "wild grapes" son to Abraham as Israel was to God.

The smell of the grapes of the choicest vine is aromatic; that of the wild grapes, pungent. The taste of the grapes of the good vine is sweet and luscious, but the taste of the wild grapes is sour and woody. In appearance, the grapes of Eshcol, the good grapes, are plump, juicy, shiny and full. Wild grapes are small, withered, worm-riddled and blighted with disease. For all his faults, Isaac brought forth a rich taste and a sweet smell, and he became a beautiful sight to the eyes of Abraham. Ishmael emitted an unpalatable flavor and a malodorous stench, and he was an eyesore in Abraham's view every time he beheld him.

Defy-Your-Parents Disagreeableness

In analyzing Ishmael's defy-your-parents rule of rebellion, the text of Genesis 16:12 next says that "his hand will be against every man." In addition to a determination to be wild, the defy-your-parents rebel is disagreeable. Regardless of the person or situation, this rule of rebellion is played out by the rebel's being against, not for or with, others. So it was that when God revealed to Abraham "the sign of circumcision, a seal of the righteousness of the faith which he had yet being uncircumcised," (Rom. 4:11), Abraham spoke to God in an intensive tone: "O that Ishmael might live before thee!" (Gen. 17:18).

This heartfelt cry of Abraham, emphasized by the interjection "O," would have been an unnecessary plea had Ishmael

been a submissive, obedient son. Such a prayer would have
been moot had not Ishmael already, and even recently, displayed disagreeable, rebellious actions. When God told
Abraham that "the uncircumcised man child…shall be cut off
from his people" (vs. 14) for breaking the covenant, no doubt
Abraham was concerned that Ishmael's disagreeable nature
might be the direct cause even of his untimely death.

Defy-Your-Parents Disapprobation

The next element of Genesis 16:12 is "every man's hand
against him." Defy-your-parents rebels move from determined
and disagreeable to disapproved. Even though he submitted outwardly to circumcision at age thirteen, he was not about to
submit inwardly to the elevation of Isaac to the position of son
of promise. On the day of Isaac's weaning, Ishmael mocked
him, and Sarah saw that mockery. Her requirement that he be
cast out was "very grievous in Abraham's sight because of his
son" (21:11); but God commanded Abraham, "In all that Sarah
hath said unto thee, hearken unto her voice" (vs. 12), and even
the hand of Ishmael's own father had to be against him.

Many people discover that co-workers or neighbors or
friends or extended family have turned against them. But God
said *every* man's hand would be against Ishmael. It is rare for a
father to have to turn against his own son, but Abraham had to
do that because Ishmael would not submit to godly, holy truth.
Ishmael was not cast out for an isolated joke against Isaac, of
course. He was cast out for a pattern of defy-your-parents
rebellion that culminated in his antagonistic mockery against
the will of God that Abraham's seed would be called through
the line of Isaac.

On the day Ishmael was cast out, "God heard the voice of
the lad; and the angel of God called to Hagar" (vs. 17). Is that
not strange? Why did God's angel talk to Hagar and not to
Ishmael? It seems plausible that God heard Ishmael's voice, but

that Ishmael was talking presumptuously, not submissively, against Abraham and Abraham's God. Therefore, God did not return answer to Ishmael, the disapproved mocker, but spoke by an angel to comfort Hagar who, in her own moment of rebellion, had received correction, returned to her mistress Sarai and submitted herself under Sarai's authority (16:6–9). Ishmael received no correction and thus procured no comfort other than to have God with him to enable him to become an archer, a man who would ever after need to rely upon his own defenses and abilities.

Defy-Your-Parents Dwelling

The next notable thing about the defy-your-parent rebel is his dwelling. Genesis 16:12 says, "And he shall dwell in the presence of all his brethren," and Genesis 21:21 adds that "he dwelt in the wilderness of Paran: and his mother took him a wife out of the land of Egypt." The dwelling of the defy-your-parents rebel is in the *wilderness* (Paran) and in the *world* (Egypt). Adherents to this type of rebellion live in a wilderness of tangled thorns and fruitless briers, of dangerous trails and perilous cliffs, of arid soils and acid earth. Such rebels live in the unmapped unknown, in the unvisited expanses of desert wastes.

Even though they dwell in the wilderness, their dwelling is always close enough to others to influence them to worldliness. Once the determined, disagreeable, disapproved, defy-your-parents rebel has been cast out, he spends the rest of his days doing all in his power to undermine righteousness in as many people as he can, especially in his own family. In order to accomplish this, he dwells "in the presence of all his brethren."

Abraham had the spiritual discernment as a father to "command his children" (18:19). After the death of Sarah, he fathered at least six sons by Keturah. The spiritual mind of this great patriarch of the faith prompted him to give "all that he had unto Isaac. But unto the sons...which [he] had, Abraham gave gifts, and sent them away from Isaac" (25:5, 6). We do not have any record of the spiritual condition of any of the sons of his concubines, but we do see that after commanding his children after him, he separated Isaac from as many unspiritual and unholy influences as possible.

Defy-Your-Parents Deficit

Finally, the defy-your-parents rebel experiences a deficit. The total of Ishmael's evidence of God's blessing was that he became an archer, and God did 'make him fruitful, and...multiplied him exceedingly...and made him a great nation' (Gen. 17:20). The contrast between that and God's blessing upon Isaac is phenomenal. The two sons received such completely different measures of the blessing of God as to be almost opposite. God's prophecy was that "Sarah thy wife shall bear thee a son indeed; and thou shalt call his name Isaac: and I will establish my covenant with him for an everlasting covenant, and with his seed after him" (vs. 19). Sarah said, "The son of this bondwoman shall not be heir with my son, even with Isaac" (21:10). All that Ishmael received was temporal talent and earthly inheritance. Isaac received eternal recognition and heavenly inheritance. As a striking indication that their blessings were separate and opposite, outside of the genealogy in I Chronicles 1:28, the only time that Isaac and Ishmael are mentioned by name in the same verse is at the funeral of their father Abraham (Gen. 25:9). Incidentally, isn't this about the only time that the godly and the ungodly get together?

Arguably, one might look to Ishmael's conception for an explanation of his defy-your-parents rebellion, because he was, in some ways, a product of rebellion. Genesis 16 records the lapse of faith of Abram and Sarai that resulted in their mutual decision for Abram to have intimate relations with Sarai's maid, Hagar, to produce the promised heir, since Sarai was barren. While God had not specifically stated yet that Sarai would be the mother of his promised Seed, God had told Abram, "He that shall come forth out of thine own bowels shall be thine heir" (15:4).

Abram's entrance in unto Hagar was mild rebellion against God's faithful promise. Both Abram and Sarai recognized this, as was evidenced once Hagar's conception was known. Sarai said, "My wrong be upon thee…the LORD judge between me and thee." (16:5). Wrongs and judgments are not the stuff of obedience and submission, but of poor decisions and unwise actions.

Furthermore, Hagar rebelled. Once she discovered herself with child by her master, Abram, she despised her mistress, Sarai. "When Sarai dealt hardly with her, she fled from her face" (vs. 6), demonstrating the rebellion she harbored in her heart against Sarai. When "the angel of the LORD found her by a fountain of water in the wilderness" (vs. 7), the angel did not sympathize with her defiance; rather, the angel told her, "Return to thy mistress, and submit thyself under her hands" (vs. 9).

It must be remembered that while parental rebellion often fosters a copycat rebellion in a child, the rebellion of a parent does not force a child to rebel. Rebellion among parents is never an honorable model to emulate or method to imitate. Rather, one ought to learn from his parents' incidents or patterns of disobedience. When the defy-your-parents rebel uses his own parents' experiences of disobedience (and no parent is perfect) to justify his own escapades into that defiance and rebellion, he is simply employing other rules of rebellion dealt with in other chapters of this book.

Illustration

A Christian couple with four children noted during the adolescent years of those children that one of them exhibited a disgruntled spirit, while the other three manifested grateful spirits. The three would be thrilled about an upcoming outing or plan, while the one would always complain. Regardless of what was going on, the three enjoyed the love of family and the blessings of togetherness, while the one groused about the favoritism in the home and despised the family unit. This one's defy-your-parents rebellion could never seem to be tamed.

When those children became adults, the three had sweet, honorable, faithful Christian families—one went to the mission field, one had a lay music position and was a devoted Christian businessman, and one taught in a Christian college. The disgruntled child? His was a lot of twice-divorced, alimony-laden, court-ruled misery. How did he cope with it? By complaining about his parents and siblings who "just didn't understand."

His defy-your-parents rebellion finally resulted in a family meeting of the three godly children along with the parents. Exasperated over the constant misrepresentations of their upbringings, they agreed to "cast out" the rebel son from the family circle rather than risk the future poisoning of their own children and the continual grieving of the parents.

The Rule That the Righteous Live By

Obedience and Honor

It is never right to defy one's parents in the spirit of Ishamel. The only time that one has biblical authority to disregard or disobey one's parents is in an instance where a parent or parents require that which is clear disobedience to God. The righteous live by the obey-and-honor rule under all other circumstances.

Ephesians 6:1–3 is the New Testament classic on this subject:

> *"Children, obey your parents in the Lord: for this is right.*
> *"Honour thy father and mother; which is the first commandment with promise;*
> *"That it may be well with thee, and thou mayest live long on the earth."*

This teaching is also found in Colossians 3:20: "Children, obey your parents in all things: for this is well pleasing unto the Lord." The rebellion that is defiant against parents is a disastrous pathway toward a life that does not go well. Indeed, "the rebellious dwell in a dry land" (Ps. 68:6).

The Ephesians and Colossians verses mention two parents: father and mother. The righteous seek no biblical permission for the divisiveness in families where a child chooses to submit to one parent while defying the other. God lists them both in the context where he commands children to obey submissively. Furthermore, the phrase "in the Lord" found in Ephesians 6:1 includes the common matter of stepparents, adoptive parents and foster parents, in addition to blood-related parents. The righteous believe in and practice the recognition of two parents in the Lord. God gives no license for a child to defy any parent unless that parent requires that which is wrong in God's sight.

The next duo found in the Ephesians portion is *two precepts:* obey and honor. Obedience is the outward conformity to command and rule and expectation, while honor is the inward heart attitude behind the obedience. It is quite possible to obey one's parents without honoring them; however, it is impossible to honor them without obeying them. Every disobedience against one's parents dishonors them; therefore, the righteous choose to honor inwardly and obey outwardly.

In the defy-your-parents culture of these last days, children have employed many excuses for disobedience. In addition to claiming the right not to obey adoptive parents or stepparents, many defiant rebels claim the idea that age eliminates the responsibility of obedience and honor. How many parents have heard a defy-your-parents rebel child say, "Come on! I'm sixteen now!" or "Why do I have to do that? I'm eighteen!" God did not give any age exemption when he told children to obey and honor their parents. He simply stated they were to do so. Obviously, a thirty-two-year-old man with a wife and four children does not have to ask his mother what brand of bath soap he should buy. However, that same man who thinks his adulthood gives him license to defy the good rules of his parents and to desecrate the good name of his parents is wrong.

In Jeremiah 35:1-10, God used a scenario to outline the type of obedience he expected from Israel and the type of parent-honoring obedience he demanded of children. God commanded the Rechabites through Jeremiah to drink wine. The sons of Rechab refused Jeremiah, saying, "We will drink no wine: for Jonadab the son of Rechab our father commanded us, saying, Ye shall drink no wine, neither ye, nor your sons for ever" (vs. 6). Interestingly, Jonadab the son of Rechab had been dead for three centuries! His great-great-great-granddescendants still obeyed him! What a testimony! And what a testimony it would be today if some children said, "My great-great-grandfather taught the ways of God, and I'm going to obey and honor him, even if he is dead and even if I am of age."

This is not the only place in Scripture where such a beautiful example of obedience is found. Esther was the queen in Ahasuerus' court, and Mordecai was merely a gatekeeper. Even so, Esther 2:20 says, "Esther did the commandment of Mordecai, like as when she was brought up with him." Let us remember that she was "adopted." For this one thing among many other honorable things that Esther did, God exalted her to great power and influence in the post-exilic age when Israel was under Medo-Persian rule.

In modern culture, one frequently hears the question of what is to be done to honor a father or mother whose very lifestyle and actions render him or her dishonorable. The answer is simple. Every child who obeys God and honors God is honoring his parents. Regardless of how ungodly a parent may be, his child honors him by obeying God. If that child obeys the unsaved parent, he may be dishonoring God. By obeying God, the child will honor both parents and God.

One final statement is needed, and that is that God never condones any type of verbal, physical, sexual or other type of parental abuse of any child. This comes under God's command to parents not to provoke their children to anger or wrath. God's requirement of obedience from children does not allow parents to exploit and hurt their children.

Finally, the text from Ephesians refers to *two promises*: living well and living still. Obeying and honoring both Dad and Mom is linked to a life that goes well. That does not mean that an obedient, honoring child will never have difficulty; rather, God means that the overall effect for the obedient, honorable child is that things go well for him. Beyond that, he lives still; that is, the influence of his life is long. Not every obedient, honorable child lives to be ninety; some, indeed, die in their youth. However, their influence is long and good. Abel has been dead longer than any other man. He did not live long, but he lived well; and he lives still, for Hebrews 11:4 says that "he being dead yet speaketh." The obedient, honorable child will have a wholesome testimony that outlives him regardless of the length of his life. Cain outlived Abel on the *calendar,* but Abel outlives Cain in his *character!*

Obedience and honor are the two things God expects of

children. Because Ishmael chose to defy his parents, he culti-vated a seed of rebellion. Had Ishmael chosen obedience and honor, he, being dead, would also still live with a heritage of believing and pleasing God.

6
The Exception-to-the-Rule Rule

"Be not deceived; God is not mocked: for whatsoever a man soweth, that shall he also reap.

"For he that soweth to his flesh shall of the flesh reap corruption; but he that soweth to the Spirit shall of the Spirit reap life everlasting."—Gal. 6:7, 8.

The chain smoker will tell you about the one individual he knows who smoked three packs a day for eighty-two years and died at ninety-four! He will not tell you about the multiplied thousands who die each year of lung cancer or other smoking-related causes in their thirties, forties and fifties—in the prime of life—who obviously smoked far less time and possibly smoked fewer packs per day. This brand of rebel lives by the exception-to-the-rule rule.

In other words, he believes that, even though ninety-nine percent of the people who embrace a particular sinful lifestyle pay a certain price, he will be able to pursue that wrong life pattern without that cost ever being exacted from him. He believes that even though ninety-nine percent of the people who follow a specific path of righteousness are rewarded with blessings both on earth and in Heaven, he should merit those same favors here and hereafter without ever following that path of righteousness. In short, the exception-to-the-rule rebel holds God to His holy promises but does not hold himself responsible for meeting the conditions to those promises.

Because the exception-to-the-rule rebel knows of some isolated individual who flirted with the rules and gambled with fate and "won," he convinces himself that he is not only somehow exempt from the consequences of his sin and wrong decisions, but that he is also somehow due the blessings and favor that would have come to him had he lived righteously and wisely. It is as if the exception-to-the-rule rebel expects God to violate His own character, disregard His own laws and create a special dispensation of treatment just for him.

Even Scripture mentions some "exceptions to the rules"; that is, some who lived parts of their lives in utter disgrace but experienced ultimate blessing. For instance, God lists four women in the lineage of Christ who had something in their lives that could damage their reputations in the eyes of some: Tamar, Rahab, Ruth and Bathsheba. Tamar seduced her father-in-law. Rahab was publicly known as a harlot. Ruth was from Moab, whose citizens were not to be allowed into God's congregation forever. Bathsheba conceived a child with one who was not her husband.

Are these "exceptions to the rule" given so that rebels will have authorization to skirt around the edges and presume to win by the rules of the rebel? No. These are given to show that God does have mercy and that any who will repent can find that mercy. God lists these examples to demonstrate that He is never boxed in by formulas but always able to extend Himself toward those who seek and find grace in His sight.

For perspective, remember that there are forty-two generations from Abraham to Christ and of those forty-two mothers in the lineage, only four are listed as having these types of ungodly things occur in their lives. That leaves an overwhelming majority of thirty-eight who were, so far as we know, godly. Furthermore, it was not the formerly incestuous Tamar, the previously whorish Rahab, the Moabite-born Ruth or the once-adulterous Bathsheba whom the Lord chose to be the human vessel for the virgin birth. God chose holy, separate, godly, humble Mary for that blessing. There are some blessings reserved for "the undefiled in the way, who walk in the law of the LORD...that keep his testimonies, and that seek him with the whole heart" (Ps. 119:1, 2).

Esau

Perhaps Esau thought that God must allow exception for him since his grandfather was Abraham, his father was Isaac and he was the firstborn in the family. When Esau was yet in the womb, God told his mother Rebekah, "Two manner of people shall be separated from thy bowels" (Gen. 25:23). When Esau and Jacob were born, they were two manner of newborns. Esau was red and hairy at birth, while the only thing said about Jacob's physical characteristics was that "his hand took hold on Esau's heel" (vs. 26).

As they grew, they remained two manner of boys. Esau's expertise was outdoor activity such as hunting and tilling the ground. Jacob contented himself and fulfilled his boyhood dreams indoors and was known as a plain man, literally meaning "gentle and pious." Apparently the rigor and strain of the harder work fell upon Esau, while the quieter and less strenuous work within the household of Isaac and Rebekah fell upon Jacob.

These two sons of Isaac were even loved differently. "Isaac loved Esau...but Rebekah loved Jacob" (vs. 28) is the assessment given about them as they continued to grow up. Scripture does not say that Isaac hated Jacob or that Rebekah hated Esau. It is evident that the boys were both loved by both parents, but that Isaac placed his devotion upon Esau while Rebekah doted upon Jacob.

All this leads to the unsurprising fact that they became two manner of men. Jacob, although a deceiver, was a man of faith. Esau, in some ways possessing a better quality of natural, worldly nobility than Jacob, was a man of fleshly scorn and rebellion. All his life, he manifested the rebellious idea that one can gamble with chance, flirt with fate, break all the rules and still somehow come to reap the blessing of having kept the rules. Esau demonstrated that he thought he could sin and come out ahead. He lived from adolescence to the end of his earthly sojourn by the exception-to-the-rule rule, deceiving himself into thinking that he could always escape the promised chastening for disobedience and that he could always receive the promised benefits as though he had kept God's ways all along.

Exception-to-the-Rule Rebellion: Esau's Despised Birthright

With regard to the birthright, it is important to note that much more is said in Scripture about the firstborn than about the birthright of the firstborn. The word "birthright" is mentioned only ten times, while the word "firstborn" occurs over one hundred times. Nevertheless, the birthright did involve the *Adamic promise* for the one who would bruise Satan's head and the *Abrahamic promise* for the one who would bless the earth. Furthermore, the birthright included double-portion inheritance rights as well as family headship and priestly rights prior to the establishment of the Aaronic priesthood.

As to God's interest in the firstborn, God called Israel His firstborn (Exod. 4:22), slew the firstborn in Egypt when Pharaoh would not let Israel go (Exod. 12:29; Ps. 78:51), sanctified the firstborn of Israel (Exod. 13:2), chose the tribe of Levi instead of the firstborn (Num. 3:45), prophesied of Christ being His firstborn (Ps. 89:27), regarded His resurrected Son as the firstborn from the dead (Col. 1:18), referred to His purchased possession as the "church of the firstborn" (Heb. 12:23) and made dozens of other general and specific references to firstborn sons. One cannot responsibly overlook the importance God placed upon this position.

The spiritual nature of the birthright of the firstborn was valuable only as the firstborn had the faith to appropriate it and the righteousness to respect it. These qualities Esau did not have; therefore, he forfeited both the familial and the spiritual benefits of being the firstborn son of Isaac of the seed of Abraham. Like Reuben, who disqualified himself in the generation of Jacob's descendants (I Chron. 5:1, 2), Esau exhibited exception-to-the-rule rebellion by neglecting the need for personal worthiness, all the while believing he could have the advantages and blessings that worthiness would bring him.

Esau's exception-to-the-rule rebellion began long before the story in Genesis 25:27–34 picked up on it; however, its first record appeared the day when Esau came in from hunting and working the fields. He was probably exhausted from the day's labors. In a premature misuse of his firstborn authority, he abruptly commanded his younger brother to feed him some of the red pottage he had cooked. Isaac was still living; therefore, Esau had no such authority over Jacob. Esau's exception-to-the-rule rebellion was revealing itself in that very instance. Scripture wastes no words, and upon this occasion God reveals that Esau, which means "hairy," was called Edom, meaning "red." Perhaps this piece of seemingly unrelated information appears here in the biblical text because Esau turned red with anger or impatience as he boldly demanded that Jacob serve him.

With respect to their names, the given name Jacob meant "supplanter," while his eventual name Israel carried the grand and glorious connotation of "prince with God." Interestingly, both names of the firstborn referred to outward things about Esau, while both names given to the secondborn had to do with inward things about Jacob. Equally important is that the second name for Esau was given by men because of Esau's carnal appetite while the second name for Jacob was assigned by God due to Jacob's spiritual appetite.

Jacob's response to his elder brother's untimely abuse of firstborn power was, "Sell me this day thy birthright" (vs. 31). Esau apathetically replied, "Behold, I am at the point to die: and what profit shall this birthright do to me?" (vs. 32). In exchanging his birthright for a bowl of red pottage, Esau proved his disdain for the spiritual value of the birthright and for the spiritual qualities that were required for one to maintain the birthright. Scripture aptly records that "thus Esau despised his birthright" (vs. 34). The despising of his birthright was but one indication of the exception-to-the-rule rebellion which he had long been developing and which he manifested in that moment when he was physically weak and spiritually unguarded.

Exception-to-the-Rule Rebellion: Esau's Disobedient Betrothals

Genesis 26 is the record of the confirmation of the Abrahamic covenant to Isaac, of Isaac's lapse and recovery of faith and of Isaac's well digging and altar building. In verse 34, Esau married two Hittite women in his second major demonstration of exception-to-the-rule rebellion. Certainly Esau knew about the miraculous provision for his father of a nonheathen wife from the right family (24:6, 7). Certainly Esau knew that Isaac's God-ordained marriage to Rebekah brought joy to his father, Abraham, and comfort to Isaac himself. Esau could easily observe the rules that his father, Isaac, had kept, and he could just as easily have kept them himself. He reasoned, however, that his life was to be the exception, that he could break the rules and still have blessing and avoid downfall.

When he began courting the wrong girls and bringing them home to the chagrin of Isaac and Rebekah, he knew what he was doing. When he decided, regardless, to marry "Judith the daughter of Beeri the Hittite, and Bashemath the daughter of Elon the Hittite: Which were a grief of mind unto Isaac and to Rebekah" (26:34, 35), he understood what he was doing. After all, Isaac and Rebekah did not wait until the wedding reception to inform Esau of their disappointment and displeasure that he had chosen as wives such wicked, worldly women. When his actions later brought his mother Rebekah to the point of such exhausted sorrow that she said, "I am weary of my life because of the daughters of Heth" (27:46), Esau had already forfeited the joy he could have had by marrying with the blessing of both God and his parents. Esau's exception-to-the-rule rebellion showed by his ill-fated betrothals and marriages that brought about the grief of disobeying the will of God rather than the joy of obedience. And Esau further demonstrated that his exception-to-the-rule rebellion could not be taught out of him even by the grief of his parents when he later married Ishmael's daughter, Mahalath (28:9), another descendant of the flesh. Esau never had the joy of family reunions and family blessing. His betrothals and marriages severed him from the possibility of those blessings and hastened him onward toward the inevitable increase of his own disillusionment and sorrow.

Exception-to-the-Rule Rebellion:
Esau's Diminished Blessing

Genesis 27:1–4 tells us that "when Isaac was old, and his eyes were dim, so that he could not see, he called Esau his eldest son, and said unto him...Behold now, I am old, I know not the day of my death: Now therefore...take me some venison;

And make me savoury meat…that I may eat; that my soul may bless thee before I die." Rebekah heard this conversation, and much of the rest of that chapter records Rebekah's unfortunate and manipulative interference into the fulfillment of the promise God had made to her that her elder son would serve her younger son.

Having surely heard rehearsings of Abraham and Sarah's disastrous effort to bring to pass the promise of an heir through Hagar and Ishmael, Rebekah knew better than to use her strength and devices to accomplish what God had previously promised he would do. In short, Rebekah led Jacob to tell several lies to the aged and blind Isaac in order to deceive Isaac into thinking Jacob was actually Esau. This accomplished, Isaac pronounced upon Jacob the Abrahamic blessing with all its firstborn birthright privileges as well as its messianic provisions, while Esau was still out hunting for the venison.

When Esau finally captured the desired animal, he dressed it and flavored it with his father's favorite herbs and spices. He probably took a bit more care than usual, all the while humming the tune of some ditty about beating the system, laughing quietly at Jacob's foolish purchase of the birthright, thinking smugly of his carnal wives and the blessing they were all about to procure. He likely engaged himself in a rather cruel chuckle of victory as he turned the meat over the fire and cooked it to the perfection of his father's preference. Esau's hope, no doubt, told a flattering tale to his soul as he carried the tender meat, still dripping with juices and steaming from the fire, to his father.

Alas, Esau's sanguine enthusiasm came to an abrupt end as he stood in the doorway of his father's chamber. Instead of seeing a hungry and eager man awaiting a celebratory meal, he saw a contented and satisfied man who had already celebrated! After the reality of this unforeseen turn of events was revealed to the two men, Isaac told Esau that someone else had come and brought him venison and that he had eaten of it and blessed him. He then concluded by saying to Esau, "And he shall be blessed" (vs. 33). Esau suddenly realized that his exception-to-the-rule rebellion had just cost him far more than he had ever intended to pay. Isaac's words were an irrevocable communication to his wayward rebel son that the blessing he had pronounced upon Jacob was irreversible and irretrievable.

Listen to Esau after he had disdained the responsibilities of his birthright, wanting only the advantages of it! Hearken to this blubbering profligate after he had disobeyed in the fundamentals of proper betrothals, desiring only the benefits of a prestigious marriage! Lend your ear to this prodigal fool after his sinful life cheated him of the high blessing which he now wanted more than anything else, but only for the sake of its power! Hear remorseful Esau as he lamented "with a great and exceeding bitter cry...Bless me, even me also, O my father....Hast thou not reserved a blessing for me...Hast thou but one blessing, my father? bless me, even me also, O my father" (vss. 34–38)!

Following this mournful plea, "Esau lifted up his voice, and wept" (vs. 38). In God's New Testament commentary upon Esau's exception-to-the-rule rebellion, Hebrews 12:17 says that Esau "found no place of repentance, though he sought [the blessing] carefully with tears." In other words, even though Esau cried bitterly, his tears were tears of regret over consequences, not of *repentance and conviction*. Esau blamed Jacob, but his blame was self-indicting. Even though Esau squeezed out a blessing from his father, it was a diminished blessing from what he could have had if he had "chosen that good part, which [could] not be taken away" (Luke 10:42) from him. Isaac did bless Esau that day with "the fatness of the earth, and of the dew of heaven" (Gen. 27:39), but this is little more than any man gets, for God "maketh his sun to rise on the evil and on the good, and sendeth rain on the just and on the unjust" (Matt. 5:45). Then Isaac told Esau that he would live by the sword, serve his brother Jacob and eventually have enough dominion to throw off the yoke of Jacob from his own neck. All this, however, was with the full knowledge of the superior blessing and birthright favor that Jacob would always possess.

Exception-to-the-Rule Rebellion: Esau's Destructive Bitterness

Esau's next exhibition of exception-to-the-rule rebellion was his design for murder. Once Esau discovered that Jacob had "stolen" the blessing by being an imposter of the first-born, he comforted himself "in his heart, [saying] The days of mourning for my father are at hand; then will I slay my brother Jacob" (Gen. 27:41). It is as though he actually believed he could reverse the promise that God had given his mother by designing the murder of Jacob so that there would be no "younger" for the "elder" to serve! Moreover, it appears that Esau thought he could commit heinous sin in killing his brother and still reap blessing from the God who had said, "Whoso sheddeth man's blood, by man shall his blood be shed: for in the image of God made he man" (9:6).

Hebrews 12:15 sheds light upon the life of this man by noting that he failed of the grace of God and allowed a "root of bitterness" to spring up to trouble him and defile many. This failure of the grace of God is by no means a loss of salvation, because Esau never expressed faith to begin with. Rather, it is a failure to appropriate the grace God made available to him to repent. Because Esau never repented, his bitterness sprang up and drove him to achieve in an I'll-show-them mentality. Yes, Esau was a man of much worldly success and power, but he was bitter.

A study of the Edomites, the descendants of Esau, shows

that this nation was by and large a heathen, pagan nation. This entire branch of the family tree of Abraham and Isaac was rooted in bitterness and rebellion, and that iniquity sprang up to visit and defile the vast majority of Esau's descendants, who then chose to follow the unsavoriness of bitter rebellion.

Exception-to-the-Rule Rebellion: Esau's Depraved Blasphemy

Hebrews 12:16 makes it plain that Esau lived his life as a profane fornicator in an ongoing demonstration of exception-to-the-rule rebellion that never came to submissive repentance. In this Holy-Ghost-inspired description of Isaac and Rebekah's elder son, we have an inside view of the man who thought he could live as an exception to the rules of piety and purity and still have the eventual outcome of a spiritual worshiper of Jehovah God.

The later years of Esau's life are passed over in obscurity. Other than the narrative of his reunion with Jacob after Jacob's twenty years with Laban in Haran, the brief statement of both sons being present at the funeral and burial of Isaac, and a listing of Esau's descendants in Genesis 36, little else is stated. An exception-to-the-rule rebel eventually passes into spiritual oblivion. Esau's biography of rebellion serves every reader as an example of what not to be and a stark reminder that those who think they can break all the rules and still win the medals are most miserably deceived.

It was Marilyn Monroe who said, "If I'd observed all the rules, I'd have never got anywhere." The grammatical deficiency aside, the blonde bombshell of the 1950s was spiritually bankrupt, as evidenced by her life of drugs, booze, immorality, divorce, depression and, eventually, probable suicide. Marilyn Monroe was an exception-to-the-rule rebel who thought rules were for everyone else, but she could disregard them and still win. Let history speak for itself.

Whether it is Esau in ancient history or Marilyn Monroe in modern history, no one can live by exception-to-the-rule rebellion and come out ahead with God in the end.

Illustration

A father made an urgent appointment with his pastor and met with him in the wee hours of a particular morning. In choked-up embarrassment, he confessed that for about a year he had been viewing pornography on the Internet. On that particular morning, his thirteen-year-old son got up with a sore throat and noticed the light shining under the computer room door. Believing that someone had inadvertently left the light on, he opened the door and found his father in the throes of perverted amusement. This father had made strict rules about the Internet for his entire family but had thought he could live as the exception to the rule.

The Rule That the Righteous Live By

Lawfulness

Paul said to Timothy, "And if a man also strive for masteries, yet is he not crowned, except he strive lawfully" (II Tim. 2:5). Paul also wrote to the Corinthians that he was "not without law to God, but under the law to Christ." Furthermore, the apostle, inspired by the Holy Spirit, went on to say that "every man that striveth for the mastery is temperate in all things" (I Cor. 9:21, 25).

Our lawless culture would have us believe that Christian liberty is the equivalent of lawlessness, but lawlessness has never been and never will be any part of God's will. Any person who would overcome exception-to-the-rule rebellion in his life and begin to please God must come to the realization that God has rules—even in the age of grace—and that He expects men to live by them!

The confusion about what law is for today and what law is not for today is partly the fault of a *lawless culture* seeking loopholes and partly the fault of *lazy clergymen* who do not study to show themselves approved to God; therefore, they cannot rightly divide the word of truth (II Tim. 2:15). There are basically three aspects of law that no longer apply to New Testament believers.

First, the *law of the Levitical priesthood of Aaron* was changed because Christ was declared "a priest for ever after the order of Melchizedek" (Ps. 110:4, quoted in Heb. 5:6; 7:17,21). The classic passage on this change is Hebrews 7:11–22. The Levitical priest was from the tribe of Levi; Christ, from the tribe of Judah. Levitical priests were ordained temporarily due to limited lifespans; Christ, forever because of His "endless life" (vs. 16). The Levitical priesthood was weak through the deaths of its priests and unprofitable through the inefficacy of its animal blood. The priesthood of Christ is strong through His resurrected glory and profitable through His redeeming, atoning blood. This entire concept is succinctly stated by Hebrews 7:12: "For the priesthood being changed, there is made of necessity a change also of the law." New Testament believers are not under the requirements of Old Testament Levitical priesthood law. That law has been changed because "Christ being come an high priest of good things to come…by his own blood [has] entered in once into the holy place, having obtained eternal redemption for us" (9:11, 12). By means of his "one sacrifice for sins for ever" (10:12), Christ "hath perfected for ever them that are sanctified" (vs. 14).

Second, Ephesians 2:15 speaks of the abolition of *the law of commandments contained in ordinances*. By comparing Ephesians 2:14–17 with Colossians 2:14, you find that this portion deals with those specific laws that separated Jews from Gentiles. Examples of this law which Christ "took…out of the way, nailing it to his cross" (Col. 2:14) include the laws of the

Passover and other feasts, the law of circumcision and the laws of clean and unclean animals. That there is no longer such a division between the Jews and the Gentiles is clear from Colossians 3:11 and Galatians 3:28. Christ has fulfilled the types in those laws, and the keeping of them today could be nothing more than ritual (I Cor. 5:7, 8; Gal. 6:15; Col. 2:14–17).

Third, the *curse of the law* has been lifted. Galatians 3:13–15 makes it plain that Christ became that curse when He hung upon the cross; that curse is no longer in force.

Other than these three aspects of law, nothing else regarding the law is ever spoken of as done away or removed. That means that there are many laws spoken of in both the Old and New Testaments and many other fuller revelations given in only the New Testament which Christians are supposed to obey. The point is that there are no exceptions to God's rules. He is merciful, long-suffering and kind, but He still has rules by which His people are to live. The righteous are law-abiding believers whose lawful striving for the mastery sets them apart for God's special use in the day of grace.

The primary law to which the righteous conform their lives is the eternal law of God. The righteous recognize spiritual law, and they conform their lives to it. Furthermore, the righteous realize that while commands may be disobeyed, God's eternal law cannot be broken. God's eternal laws are His never-changing means of dealing with mankind.

In his sermon, "It's About Time," from the book entitled *When God Breaks Through*, Vance Havner said, "You can't break the law of God. Nobody ever broke the law of God. You break yourself against the law of God. You might as well attack Gibralter with a popgun as to go up against the law of God in your own little weak self. You can't do it. You can't jump over a skyscraper. You don't break the law of gravity. You can break your neck—but break the law of gravity? And there are those today who think they can be immoral and escape the consequences."

For example, God has a law that says, "Whatsoever a man soweth, that shall he also reap" (Gal. 6:7). This spiritual law is closely akin to another one that reads, "He which soweth sparingly shall reap also sparingly; and he which soweth bountifully shall reap also bountifully" (II Cor. 9:6). No man has ever broken one of these laws. The righteous who strive lawfully and who live under the law to Christ will organize their lives around this law and submit to its applications, whether in sowing of *time, talent, truth* or *tithe.*

Another of God's laws says "God resisteth the proud, but giveth grace unto the humble" (Jas. 4:6). This is a beautiful law, and the righteous who are seeking to strive temperately for the mastery live by it, rejoice in it and benefit from it. Exception-to-the-rule rebels think they can press on in pride and then have the grace of God on their terms whenever they want it. God, however, has a law that no man has ever broken, and that law states that He resists those proud ones and reserves His grace for the humble.

One more tenet of spiritual law is that "there is no respect of persons with God" (Rom. 2:11). This particular law is worded in a variety of ways in eight separate Bible references. All eight of them are in contexts involving a holy respect for God and His unchanging dealings with man. The righteous who desire to live under the law to Christ will shape their lives around this law; exception-to-the-rule rebels will seek just as diligently to wrench themselves away from it. God declares that this simple law should govern the act of judging (II Chron. 19:7; Prov. 24:23, 28:21), leadership as an employer (Eph. 6:9; Col. 3:25), feelings toward the rich and poor (Jas. 2:1) and evaluating works (I Pet. 1:17). The righteous allow this law to affect them in a good way.

Beyond such all-encompassing laws, God has specific commands by which the righteous live. Consider some of these examples.

"Wherefore receive ye one another, as Christ also received us to the glory of God."—Rom. 15:7.

"Therefore judge nothing before the time, until the Lord come."—I Cor. 4:5.

"Be perfect, be of good comfort, be of one mind, live in peace."—II Cor. 13:11.

"Bear ye one another's burdens."—Gal. 6:2.

"Be renewed in the spirit of your mind."—Eph. 4:23.

"Stand fast in the Lord, my dearly beloved."—Phil. 4:1.

"Take heed to the ministry which thou hast received in the Lord, that thou fulfil it."—Col. 4:17.

"Prove all things; hold fast that which is good."—I Thess. 5:21.

"Brethren, be not weary in well doing."—II Thess. 3:13.

"Follow after righteousness, godliness, faith, love, patience, meekness."—I Tim. 6:11.

"Be not thou therefore ashamed of the testimony of our Lord."—II Tim. 1:8.

"Put them in mind to be subject to principalities and powers, to obey magistrates, to be ready to every good work,

"To speak evil of no man, to be no brawlers, but gentle, shewing all meekness unto all men."—Titus 3:1, 2.

"Refresh my bowels in the Lord."—Philem. 20.

"Cast not away therefore your confidence."—Heb. 10:35.

> "*Swear not, neither by heaven, neither by the earth, neither by any other oath: but let your yea be yea; and your nay, nay.*"—Jas. 5:12.

> "*Have fervent charity among yourselves.*"—I Pet. 4:8.

> "*Give diligence to make your calling and election sure.*"—II Pet. 1:10.

> "*Little children, keep yourselves from idols.*"—I John 5:21.

> "*Look to yourselves, that we lose not those things which we have wrought, but that we receive a full reward.*"—II John 8.

> "*Beloved, follow not that which is evil, but that which is good.*"—III John 11.

> "*Remember ye the words which were spoken before of the apostles of our Lord Jesus Christ.*"—Jude 17.

This is a random selection of one command from each New Testament epistle, and it is such commands by which the righteous live. The righteous live lawfully, spurning the mentality that says they are the exceptions. Righteous believers know that God moves as He deems right and just and that His movements are not always according to their rhyme and reason. They do not presume upon that God who is right and just and expect His blessing upon lawlessness. The righteous choose to dwell within the boundaries of His eternal, spiritual, moral law, living lawfully all their days.

7
The I-Don't-Care-How-Much-I-Hurt-You Rule

"Thy wickedness may hurt a man as thou art; and thy righteousness may profit the son of man."—Job 35:8.

Rebels have an agenda, and that agenda brings hurt—often irreversible and irreparable—to others. While no one can see the heart of another man, it is seldom that a rebel seems to care about the degree of pain or even the pain itself that he causes to others. In all justice to the rebel, he may or may not plan the hurt that results because of his callousness toward the Spirit of God. Many a rebel has been heard to say that he never intended to hurt anyone. While it may be noble to say that no harm was intended, it is nobler to live so that no harm is incurred. Enough harm comes to people due to nothing more than the curse of sin upon this world, without more harm caused by the selfishness and stubbornness of I-don't-care-how-much-I-hurt-you rebels.

Joseph's Brethren

Joseph's ten brothers demonstrate this rule of rebels. Joseph was the favored son of Israel. His coat of many colors indicated that he was the son chosen not only for the Hebrew birthright but also for the Abrahamic blessing. However, Joseph was not chosen merely by his earthly father, Israel

(Jacob's God-given name). His God and Heavenly Father had also chosen Joseph to special service, as his adolescent dreams clearly attested. This, of course, was seen by the discerning, Spirit-led mind of Israel, his father; however, Joseph's brothers did not have spiritual minds. When Joseph communicated the substance of his dreams to his family, his brothers "envied him; but his father observed the saying" (Gen. 37:11). Israel perceived that his aspiring young son was sanctified for a unique ministry and service, but all that his brothers thought about was an opportunity to topple Joseph from his seat of future jurisdiction.

Having received a command from his father in Genesis 37:13, 14 to travel to Shechem to search out the well-being of his ten older brothers and their flocks, Joseph obeyed. Upon seeing Joseph coming, the ten brothers first conspired to kill him, cast him into a pit and report that "some evil beast hath devoured him" (vs. 20). Such a plan, had it hatched, would have caused deep, irreversible pain to Jacob, Benjamin and any other concerned person in the family. This rule of rebels is demonstrated when we see that the prospect of that calibre of pain did not enter the conversation. There was not one of the ten brothers who spoke up to say, "Hey, wait a minute! We need to think about what this would do to Dad and Benjamin and Aunt Leah!"

Reuben, whose firstborn status had been jeopardized by his inappropriate defilement of his father's concubine, Bilhah (35:22, 49:4), evidently saw this as a prime opportunity to recapture the good graces of his father. Therefore, he recommended that Joseph be cast into a pit but not murdered. His unwritten agenda was to go to that pit in the night, lift Joseph out and secretly return him to Jacob with the gallant tale of how he had delivered him from his evil brothers' murder plot. This effort failed, however, because while Reuben was absent, Judah hatched the idea to sell Joseph to Midianite merchantmen for twenty pieces of silver. Genesis 37:27 relates that the brothers were "content" with this plan. Reuben lamented, wailing, "The child is not; and I, whither shall I go?" (vs. 30). The ten boys then killed a young goat, dipped Joseph's multicolored coat in its blood and took that blood-stained garment home to their father. They told him, "This have we found: know now whether it be thy son's coat or no" (vs. 32).

The outward show of rent clothing, many days in sackcloth and inconsolable tears were but symbolic of the inner rending of Israel's heart. Scripture reports that "all his sons [Benjamin included this time] and all his daughters rose up to comfort him; but he refused to be comforted; and he said, For I will go down into the grave unto my son mourning" (vs. 35). One must wonder what sort of pretense these ten brothers utilized in attempting to express comfort to their father, when they and their evil deed were the cause of his grief. Why, as days of mourning strung out into weeks and months and years, did not even one of them ever break the code of silence and come clean? Not even Reuben's yearning to be reconciled to the place of the firstborn was enough to prompt him to bring an end to Israel's sorrow. They did not care how much they hurt Israel. Rebels never care about the pain they cause.

Nor does the story end here. The ten older sons of Israel did not care how much they hurt Benjamin. As the only full-blooded brother, Joseph's mysterious disappearance must have affected him deeply. Joseph and Benjamin had a bond that they did not share with the others. The loss of his beloved brother must have left scars upon Benjamin that, though they aren't expressly penned in Scripture, were certainly etched into Benjamin's soul. It is hardly possible that those older brothers did not see that pain in their youngest sibling's countenance, but they did not care enough to do anything about it. The rule is that rebels don't care how much they hurt others.

But wait. The story is not over. Those ten brothers hurt Joseph too. All throughout Genesis 39 and following, even a casual reader can see how the Lord was with Joseph, blessing him, protecting him, helping him. Joseph was seventeen when he set out on his father's errand (37:2) and thirty when he stood before Pharaoh (41:46). Thirteen years had elapsed. Add to that the seven years of plenty that followed and the two years of famine before Joseph revealed himself to his brothers and was ultimately reunited with his father, and you see that for twenty-two years, Joseph hurt! But his brothers cared too little to do anything about it.

What transpired in Joseph's meditations while he was being hauled off by the Ishmeelites that fateful night when he narrowly escaped death? What thoughts raced through his mind as he stood shackled to an auction block while people whose language he could not understand bid upon his worth? What apprehension did Joseph experience when a burly Egyptian yanked him free from the thongs that held his hands and feet and abruptly shoved him toward Potiphar, the highest bidder? What revulsion did he feel during the insulting, insidious temptations thrown at him by Potiphar's wife? What did Joseph ponder in the undeserved shame, unkempt conditions and unwarranted mockeries he most definitely underwent in a foreign jail? How great was his agony when he was forgotten by the butler and baker?

Did his brothers care? No. And while Scripture does not tell us this specifically, it is unrealistic to believe that Joseph was unaffected. What the Bible does say is that, at long last, Joseph was brought before Pharaoh. During the seven years of plenty, Joseph was married and became the father of two sons, Manasseh and Ephraim. Their names meant "forgetting" and "fruitful" respectively. Joseph named them thus, saying, "God…hath made me forget all my toil, and all my father's house. And…God hath caused me to be fruitful in the land of my affliction" (41:51, 52). He came to this level of acceptance after fifteen to twenty years, but it is hardly questionable that Joseph had endured multiplied nights of inconsolable weeping and myriad days of confused wondering in the process.

Then the Word of God tells us that when he was finally reunited with his brothers after twenty-two years, he said, "So now it was not you that sent me hither, but God" (45:8). He came to such a disciplined and mature conclusion after twenty-two years, but he most certainly did not always have such a victorious mind-set. Furthermore, after Israel's death, he told them all, "But as for you, ye thought evil against me; but God meant it unto good, to bring to pass, as it is this day, to save much people alive" (50:20). This fabulous statement from Joseph's lips is the Romans 8:28 of the Old Testament, but it was spoken seventeen years later still, nearly forty years after the onset of this story of Joseph's hurt and pain.

Let us note, in discussing Joseph's pain, what Joseph did not say in naming Manasseh. He did not say that he had forgotten his father. No, he had forgotten his father's house; that is, his older brothers who had served him so ill. But how he must have hurt for his father who had so devotedly loved him! Manasseh or no Manasseh, Joseph's heart ached every day for all those years for his beloved father. Joseph did not say in naming Ephraim that his dreams had come true. His dreams must have mocked him on some occasions and confused him on others. For all those years, Joseph hurt because of the vanishing of his dreams.

When Joseph finally revealed himself to his brothers, he did not say that his brothers had not hurt him. He simply told them he had learned how to deal with the hurt. After Israel's death, Joseph's brothers "sent a messenger unto Joseph, saying, Thy father did command before he died, saying, So shall ye say unto Joseph, Forgive, I pray thee now, the trespass of thy brethren, and their sin; for they did unto thee evil: and now, we pray thee, forgive the trespass of the servants of the God of thy father" (Gen. 50:16, 17). They did not even go to Joseph themselves. They sent a messenger!

They called Israel "thy father," not "our father," manifesting the distance between Joseph and them. Perhaps Israel did command this, but perhaps this was another lie that all ten agreed to promote to save themselves for the next stage of life. At any rate, they worded it as a command from Israel to add gravity to it in the hopes that Joseph would obey what they portrayed as his dying father's wishes. What cowardice! Did they even yet care about the pain they had caused Joseph? One wonders.

Again, Joseph did not tell his brothers they had not hurt him. In fact, he plainly told them they were evil in their intentions, while he extolled the Lord whose ways are so high and great that He can use even the wrath of man to accomplish His glories.

The beautiful thing about the story of Joseph is that, even though rebels do not care how much they hurt the participants and bystanders in their lives, God does care! Even when rebels go on in *careless apathy* while someone else endures *ceaseless agony*, God steps in to care! And even after all those years and all that pain and all the unnecessary troubles, God can enable the one who is hurt to forgive and move on. God cares, but rebels do not, and that is a rule that rebels keep close to their hearts.

King Herod

Matthew's gospel account is unique in giving the record of the wise men who traveled from the East to Jerusalem in search of the Christ child. Their question in the streets of the Jewish capital city as to the whereabouts of the one "born King of the Jews" (Matt. 2:2) troubled Herod and brought turmoil to the entire city. The resulting conference between Herod and the chief priests and scribes produced the solution that Christ would be born in Bethlehem in accord with the words of the prophet Micah.

This bit of information caused Herod to call the wise men back so he could send them to Bethlehem to bring the Child to Jerusalem where he could "worship" Him as well. Thus, the wise men were dispatched upon the final leg of their journey. They arrived at the house where Joseph and Mary lived with Christ, and there they offered gifts and bowed in worship to Jesus Christ, the incarnate Son of God.

God, knowing the mendacious plot of Herod to kill Christ, warned the wise men not to return to Jerusalem or to Herod. This foiling of his sinister plan brought Herod to great wrath, and in another biblical account of I-don't-care-how-much-I-hurt-you rebellion, he "sent forth, and slew all the children that were in Bethlehem, and in all the coasts thereof, from two years old and under" (vs. 16). Can one imagine what pain this brought to that community! Even though Bethlehem was "little among the thousands of Judah" (Mic. 5:2), it contained loving fathers and mothers, hope-filled grandfathers and grandmothers, happy and delighted brothers and sisters and devoted extended family members. The slaughter of these innocents brought pain of such intensity to this community and the surrounding area that it is likely that many other connected ills and related difficulties developed in the months and years following. No wonder Jeremiah foretold of that day, saying, "A voice was heard in Ramah, lamentation, and bitter weeping; Rahel weeping for her children refused to be comforted for her children, because they were not" (Jer. 31:15). Did Herod care? No. This type of rebel never cares how much others hurt.

Illustration

A faithful Christian couple had a son and twin daughters one year younger. The son showed signs of rebellion by age fifteen, and to the chagrin of his parents, he became incorrigible. The boy defiled his home time after time in tirades of rebellious insults, leaving his mother dissolved in tears and his father to discouraged torments. They sent him at age sixteen to a Christian boys' home in their city, but even the efforts of trained Christians failed despite dozens of counseling sessions and firm discipline. He was eventually dismissed at age seventeen. On the night of his dismissal, he did not go home. Instead, he called two of his rebel buddies from the past, and with them he headed to a nearby dive in a borrowed car for a night of revelry. On the way, he wrecked the car and was left paralyzed from the neck down. His two friends were both killed.

The medical bills mounted. The father who had frugally saved to send all three of his children to a Christian college lost both his savings and his house. The mother suffered a nervous breakdown. After helping care for their mother until she recovered, the two faithful daughters had to pay their own way through college, enduring many hardships because of it. To the glory of God, the parents and daughters are all still faithfully serving God and will all testify that God has shown them great truths and much blessing.

The son? To the moment of this writing, he has never offered one word of sorrow for his sin to his father, to his mother, to his sisters, to any of the family members of his two friends nor to the owner of the borrowed car. He continues to live by the rule that rebels do not care how much pain they cause other people.

The Rule That the Righteous Live By

Compassion

Whether we're dealing with Joseph's brothers, Herod or a hundred other rebels whose sin and iniquity have brought unnecessary pain to millions, the Scriptural solution is compassion. The primary ingredient of a righteous character that is missing from the I-don't-care-how-much-I-hurt-you rebels is compassion. God once asked, "Can a woman forget her sucking child, that she should not have compassion on the son of her womb?" (Isa. 49:15), and in that verse God answered His own question with the word "yea." God was explaining how it is possible for I-don't-care-how-much-I-hurt-you rebels to inflict undeserved pain upon the unwary around them. If even a mother can forget her own infant, certainly flint-hearted men can exhibit a compassionless spirit toward those who are around them.

The righteous live by the rule of compassion. First and foremost, God Himself has compassion; indeed, He is compassion personified. Think of His centuries of long-suffering compassion with Israel. One of a number of passages that could be cited is II Chronicles 36:15, where the Bible says, "The LORD God of their fathers sent to them by his messengers, rising up betimes, and sending; because he had compassion on his people, and on his dwelling place." What might have happened to Israel had God not possessed perfect and complete compassion? Israel might well have ceased to exist even before they got to Canaan. He might well have wiped them out as He told Moses He would do.

However, because "his compassions fail not" and "are new every morning" (Lam. 3:22, 23), God had mercy. Indeed, God, "being full of compassion, forgave their iniquity, and destroyed them not: yea, many a time turned he his anger away, and did not stir up all his wrath" (Ps. 78:38). All this testifies to the fact that our Lord is "a God full of compassion, and gracious, longsuffering, and plenteous in mercy and truth" (86:15). The rule the righteous live by is compassion, a compassion instilled by God that purposely sets out to prevent needless pain upon unwary bystanders and to alleviate or eliminate needless pain that has already been inflicted.

God is our Pattern in His compassion toward the individual also. "Unto the upright there ariseth light in the darkness: he is gracious, and full of compassion, and righteous" (112:4). The righteous live uprightly, and out of God's inner nature, He visits their souls with light in the darkness. His graciousness, compassion and righteousness are similar and complementary qualities, and they all cooperate in God's dealings with the righteous who live by the right rules.

In His earthly ministry, the Son of God manifested compassion on the multitudes (Matt. 9:36; 15:32), upon the blind (20:34), upon the lepers (Mark 1:41), upon the demoniacs (5:19; 9:22) and upon the helplessly bereaved (Luke 7:13). Even more than any Levitical priest, as our Great High Priest He has "compassion on the ignorant, and on them that are out of the way" (Heb. 5:2). Even though He is not Himself a sinner or one bound by infirmity like the Aaronic priests were, He is "touched with the feeling of our infirmities" (4:15), and what is that, if it is not compassion? The righteous live by the rule of compassion because Jesus had compassion. He "went about doing good" (Acts 10:38), alleviating pain, not originating new pain and aggravating existing pain as one without compassion.

Think what happened at the banks of the Nile River when Pharaoh's daughter opened the little ark wherein the baby Moses was lying. "The babe wept. And she had compassion on him" (Exod. 2:6), causing her to attend to his comforts and needs rather than neglect him and inflict further pain upon the innocent child. Pharaoh himself was a hardhearted, compassionless tyrant whose soul was so calloused as to care not for the pain he caused all those Hebrew parents who bore boys. His daughter, however, had a different heart, a compassionate one; and her act of compassion ended up delivering the nation her father intended to destroy! The righteous live by the rule of compassion, because in doing so, they can actually undo the heartlessness of I-don't-care-how-much-I-hurt-you rebels.

Four specific Bible verses emphasize this precious rule by which the righteous live. The first is Hebrews 10:34, where the believers "had compassion of [him] in [his] bonds, and took joyfully the spoiling of [their] goods." The righteous who live by the rule of compassion actually endure personal pain to ensure that others do not have to. The situation of the author of Hebrews is mysterious here. Regardless of his circumstances, the believers actually allowed their own possessions to be plundered in their compassionate dedication to meeting his needs. These Christians who lived by the righteous rule of compassion came close to emulating Aquila and Priscilla, of whom Paul said "[They] have for my life laid down their own necks" (Rom. 16:4).

The second verse that describes the rule of compassion by which the righteous live is I Peter 3:8, where the apostle Peter enjoins his readers, "Finally, be ye all of one mind, having compassion one of another, love as brethren, be pitiful, be courteous." The next verse forbids returning evil for evil and requires returning blessing in order that God may bless. The righteous will demonstrate compassion to the point of dear personal cost and under the conditions of being maligned and persecuted. I-don't-care-how-much-I-hurt-you rebels will inflict pain upon people who just happen to be in the way, and even more pain upon people who hurt them. The righteous do not return hurt for hurt because their compassion disallows such recompense.

Finally, God speaks of the rule of compassion that the righteous employ in soul winning. Jude 22, 23 say,

> *"And of some have compassion, making a difference:*
> *"And others save with fear, pulling them out of the fire."*

The ultimate pain that is inflicted by I-don't-care-how-much-I-hurt-you rebels is the pain of the tormenting flames of an eternal Hell. Rebels are self-serving individuals who could not be bothered with getting the soul-saving Gospel into the hands and ears and hearts of the unsaved. By their neglect, rebels actually bring eternal pain to some whom they might otherwise reach! The righteous live by the rule of compassion, going after the souls of lost men, women, boys and girls in an effort to bring them to salvation. Indeed, the righteous "endure all things for the elect's sakes, that they may also obtain the salvation which is in Christ Jesus with eternal glory" (II Tim. 2:10).

8
The I-Will-Not-Admit-Defeat Rule

"A prudent man foreseeth the evil, and hideth himself: but the simple pass on, and are punished."—Prov. 22:3.

Rebels are always in line to receive their due eventually. When that just result finally arrives, rebels will occasionally back down and take stock and alter their lives to prevent further retribution. However, some rebels simply will not back down. There is a rebel who absolutely will not stop his sin, because to do so is to admit that the righteous are right and that the rebellious are wrong. The obstinacy of I-will-not-admit-defeat rebels is unrivaled. They press on in their rebellion to the bitter end.

Pharaoh

During the days of the sojourn of the children of Israel in Egypt, "there arose up a new king over Egypt, which knew not Joseph" (Exod. 1:8). This king, unaware of the riches that the Israelites had brought to the nation of Egypt and unconcerned about the covenant of Jehovah with them, became concerned with the rapid numerical growth of the descendants of Abraham. He surmised that the tail would soon be wagging the dog and that he should take some decisive action. Thus Pharaoh did several things in his intimidating, conniving effort to ensure that the dog would continue wagging the tail.

First, he enslaved the children of Israel, employing them in rigorous labor. When that resulted in their proliferation rather than their diminishment, he devised a plan to murder the boy babies during childbirth. God intervened in this situation, giving the Jewish women quick births before the midwives even arrived. Seeing that his plan had been foiled again, the king commanded that every newborn son be cast into the Nile River, "in which time Moses was born, and was exceeding fair...And when he was cast out, Pharaoh's daughter took him up, and nourished him for her own son" (Acts 7:20, 21).

The narratives of Exodus and Acts quickly move from the birth of Moses to his adulthood. "And when he was full forty years old, it came into his heart to visit his brethren the children of Israel" (vs. 23). Upon arrival at one of the labor camps where the enslaved Israelites were in forced toil, he observed an Egyptian abusing one of his brethren, and in a sudden response to injustice, "he slew the Egyptian, and hid him in the sand" (Exod. 2:12). The explanation for Moses' intervention is not given in Exodus, but Acts 7:25 says that "he supposed his brethren would have understood how that God by his hand would deliver them: but they understood not."

The next day, it was not an insult between an Egyptian and a Hebrew that he attempted to settle, but a strife between two of his own nation. The two who were at odds reacted with anger, asking Moses who he thought he was and whether he intended to kill one of them too. When Moses heard that his unintentional murder was public knowledge, he fled to Midian. During Moses' years in Midian, that oppressive dictator who first decided to crush the Hebrew "threat" died, and Moses himself married and had two sons.

"And when forty [more] years were expired, there appeared to [Moses] in the wilderness of mount Sina an angel of the Lord in a flame of fire in a bush" (vs. 30). At this meeting, God commissioned Moses to return to Egypt and deliver his brethren, giving him among other assurances the fact that "all the men are dead which sought thy life" (Exod. 4:19). The death of the first oppressive Pharaoh did not eliminate the dictatorial trend, however, and when Moses arrived back in Egypt to lead out the Hebrews with the rallying cry of "let my people go," he met with an I-will-not-admit-defeat type of rebel who just happened to occupy the most powerful throne in the world for that time.

Most readers of Scripture are at least somewhat familiar with the story of the Exodus of the Hebrews from Egypt. Seldom, however, is the story viewed with enough detail to see how unbelievably stubborn Pharaoh actually was and how his own court and his own people gradually came to sympathize with Moses' cause. In fact, once the Lord severed the land of Goshen from the rest of Egypt, the Hebrews' suffering subsided drastically, while the Egyptians' suffering increased tremendously. One can also see that Pharaoh's intense fury and unrelenting determination to win against Jehovah drove him to what is possibly history's most senseless story of I-will-not-admit-defeat rebellion. For one who was raised up by God in order to demonstrate God's power and spread God's name through all the earth (Exod. 9:16; Rom. 9:17), he most certainly missed the boat. Although he unintentionally caused the name of Jehovah to be spread all through Egypt, his I-will-not-admit-defeat rebellion brought such destruction to his people and nation that it prevented their ever enjoying God's power or using it for beneficent purposes.

At first, the effect upon Egypt was minimal. Moses' rod-turned-serpent devoured the magicians' rods that had also become serpents. The only difficulty here was that the magicians had to train new asps for their court functions and soothsaying chicanery. The next day, when Moses turned the waters of Egypt to blood, however, the damaging effect of

I-will-not-admit-defeat rebellion took on a new dimension. Now "all the Egyptians [had to dig] round about the river for water to drink; for they could not drink of the water of the river" (Exod. 7:24). This unsavory situation prevailed for seven days. Imagine how much additional work was required of everyone in the kingdom. Consider all the backbreaking labor that was added to the already-taxed Hebrews whose toil and labor was at the breaking point. Pharoah's rebellion against Jehovah manifested itself in the fact that he would win at any cost.

Next came the frogs, filling bedchambers and kneading troughs with their slimy bodies and their incessant croakings and gurglings. When the frogs died, the damage included the additional work of gathering their carcasses together into heaps, the nauseating stench so common to dead water creatures, the spread of disease from the rotting carcasses, and the work of final disposal. Did Pharaoh relent? No. His rebellion was the type that simply would not admit defeat regardless of the inconvenience imposed and the glaring evidence that he had, indeed, been beaten.

After the frogs came the lice. This time, Pharaoh's magicians came to the end of their copycatting, openly admitting that turning dust to lice was "the finger of God" (8:19) in a mild but obvious attempt to persuade Pharaoh to soften. Pharaoh did not soften. He hardened. He would not admit defeat even though his own masters of witchcraft were rendered irrelevant by the superior power of God. The entire nation suffered with lice upon both man and beast. Not only were the people afflicted with bites and welts and incessant itching, but the animals were driven to crazed stampeding so common among flocks and herds that are infested with insect pests. It is even likely that the plague of lice adversely affected the milk production of cows, sheep and goats so that both the animal offspring that were nursing as well as the people who were dependent upon milk for nourishment were deprived. Did Pharoah back down? No. His I-will-not-admit-defeat rebellion against the Lord was so indelibly etched into his flint-hard heart that he could not be bothered with the obvious defeat of and damage to even his own people.

Following the lice, the Lord sent swarms of flies. This time, he separated the land of Goshen where His people lived, sending this and all subsequent plagues upon the Egyptians only and delivering the long-oppressed Hebrews from the suffering. The degree of this plague is recognizable in that "there came a grievous swarm of flies...[and] the land was corrupted by reason of the swarm of flies" (vs. 24). The word "corrupted" implies that this insect invasion brought diseases to the people. Pharaoh did not mellow. His rebellion was the type that simply would not admit defeat even if agony and distress were all around him. His rebellion would triumph and never cave!

Moses next brought a plague known as a murrain, an infectious disease of cattle. The Egyptian people, along with all peoples of history, depended largely upon their animals for luxuries and daily needs ranging from transportation to field work to food. The disease and death of "all the cattle of Egypt" (9:6) brought unprecedented hardship and disaster upon the subjects of this radical, unthinking tyrant whose rebellion against Jehovah would not stop for anything. Even the prospect of poverty that would, of necessity, be the outcome of such a national epidemic did not moderate his rebellion. This plague likely brought difficulties to the Hebrews also, because even though not one of the cattle of the children of Israel died, the Egyptians may well have stolen away many of the Hebrews' cattle, since two plagues later, "he that feared the word of the LORD among the servants of Pharaoh made his servants and his cattle flee into the houses" (vs. 20). They had apparently replenished their dead flocks and herds from some source.

After the murrain, God sent boils from the ashes of the furnace. These boils were the type that broke forth with blains, and again this plague was upon all men and beasts. Blains are serum-filled blisters that arise up under the skin and then burst under slight pressure. So painful they were that Pharaoh's "magicians could not stand before Moses because of the boils" (vs. 11), but Pharaoh's untiring I-will-not-admit-defeat rebellion led him to harden despite this unleashing of God's anger against him.

After the boils came the hail. The servants of Pharaoh who had come to see the power of God brought their cattle under safe cover, but they could not save their crops. The flax and barley were destroyed, and the fruit trees were broken, leaving Egypt and all of its people with the prospect of near-famine condition and possible starvation, but Pharaoh's I-will-not-admit-defeat rebellion surged forward without abatement.

Pharaoh's servants, swooning in pain from boils, fearing the impending famine from the crop destruction and realizing they were defeated, pleaded with Pharaoh, "How long shall [Moses] be a snare unto us? let the men go…knowest thou not yet that Egypt is destroyed?" (10:7). Pharaoh was not appeased. Not even the hard evidence all about him combined with the sound advice of his trusted lords could mollify his stubbornness.

Hard on the heels of the hail and its vegetative destruction, God brought the plague of locusts to finish the job. This locust plague was of such magnitude that Egyptian history had no parallel. They blocked out the sun from the land, and they left nothing behind in all the land of Egypt.

Three days of utter pitch darkness then covered the land. Imagine the difficulty this brought to all. Nothing could be done. Accidental injuries and even deaths could have easily occurred. No one could see. It was as if the entire nation were blind for three days, but Pharaoh stood fast in his rebellion. He did not slacken. He was Pharaoh, the Morning and the Evening Star, the I-will-not-admit-defeat emperor of Egypt. They were but his subjects and his servants. The plagues would soon end, he was sure.

But wait. The I-will-not-admit-defeat rebel does think of himself. When his rebellion squeezes the blood from his own heart, he relents. When the darkness ended, God visited his people Israel and told them of the Passover. Once the Jews had sacrificed the Passover and stricken the doorpost and lintel with blood, and once the Lord had passed through the land and destroyed "the firstborn of Pharaoh that sitteth upon his throne, even unto the firstborn of the maidservant that is behind the mill" (11:5), the I-will-not-admit-defeat rebel broke down. He let the people go. He sent them on their way.

It would seem likely to one unfamiliar with Bible history that this might have been the end of the story, but it wasn't. Fresh back from his own son's funeral, Pharaoh's I-will-not-admit-defeat rebellion immediately resurfaced, filling his vengeful, hardened heart again, and "he made ready his chariot, and...took six hundred chosen chariots, and....pursued after them....and overtook them encamping by the sea" (14:6–9). Unwilling to endure a permanent softening and unaware of the finality of his reckless rashness, Pharaoh risked his entire army's lives by pursuing Israel between the walls of the congealed waters of the Red Sea. God reached down and *hastened* the progress of the Hebrews while He *hindered* the progress of the Egyptians. When the Hebrews reached the safety of high ground, Moses lifted up his rod, and the waters returned in full strength; and "Israel saw the Egyptians dead upon the sea shore" (vs. 30). The end result of Pharaoh's I-will-not-admit-defeat rebellion was that, after he had occasioned the hopeless defeat of all the gods of Egypt and incredibly refused to be stopped even by the sorrow of his own son's death, he condemned himself and his entire army to the eternal pain and torment of death in Hell. Truthfully, this is the ultimate defeat of all rebellion, even of I-will-not-admit-defeat rebellion. Whether or not such rebels admit it, they are eventually defeated.

Nebuchadnezzar

The rise of Babylon's most truculent dictator is concealed from Bible history. Suffice it to say that he came out of "nowhere" to lead the Babylonian Empire to its governmental, territorial and military heights. The earthly writers of the Books of Kings and Chronicles give some brief insight into this man. Habakkuk alludes to him in Habakkuk 2:4, 5 and then in the rest of the chapter prophesies five woes upon this audacious and formidable ruler. Jeremiah mentions Nebuchadnezzar by name over three dozen times, usually with the alternate spelling of Nebuchadrezzar, but it is the prophet Daniel who gives the most accurate details about this ruthless emperor with over thirty references to him in only five chapters. Nebuchadnezzar was an I-will-not-admit-defeat rebel whose story has a happier ending than Pharaoh's.

I Will Not Admit Defeat by Evidence

Daniel 1 details the account of the original captivity of "certain of the children of Israel, and of the king's seed, and of the princes; Children in whom was no blemish, but well favoured, and skilful in all wisdom, and cunning in knowledge, and understanding science, and such as had ability in them to stand in the king's palace, and whom they might teach the learning and the tongue of the Chaldeans" (vss. 3, 4), among whom four were specifically named: Daniel, Hananiah, Mishael and Azariah (vs. 6). The first command of Nebuchadnezzar to the prince of the eunuchs was to change their Hebrew names to Babylonian names and to acquaint these youngsters with

Babylonian foods, drink and customs.

Daniel's famous 'purpose of heart' (vs. 8), which one can assume was also the purpose of heart of his three friends, resulted in the concern of Melzar (the immediate superior of Daniel and his friends) that they might not appear healthy when they stood before the king, and that he, therefore, might be beheaded for improper care of these treasured captives. Daniel asked to be proven for just ten days, and the result of their eating proper foods was "countenances [that] appeared fairer and fatter in flesh than all the children which did eat the portion of the king's meat" (vs. 15). The text goes on to report that God gave to Daniel and his three friends "knowledge and skill in all learning and wisdom," and that God gave singularly to Daniel "understanding in all visions and dreams" (vs. 17). When the king examined all the captives at the end of the probation period, "among them all was found none like Daniel, Hananiah, Mishael, and Azariah: therefore stood they before the king" (vs. 19). In fact, they were "ten times better than all the magicians and astrologers that were in all [Nebuchadnezzar's] realm" (vs. 20). Did Nebuchadnezzar admit defeat? Did he make drastic changes in his court, weeding out the incompetent counselors and satanic necromancers? Did the evidence of the superiority of Jehovah presented by Daniel, Hananiah, Mishael and Azariah persuade or convince Nebuchadnezzar to admit the defeat of his dumb idols and the puppet prophets of his court? No. Nebuchadnezzar was an I-will-not-admit-defeat rebel.

I Will Not Admit Defeat by Embarrassment

In Daniel's second chapter, God gives the story of Nebuchadnezzar's dream of the great image. When Nebuchadnezzar awoke from this dream, he found that he could neither understand nor retrieve the dream. The dream was gone. Did he call Daniel, Hananiah, Mishael and Azariah, the ten-times-better scholars from Judea? No. This I-will-not-admit-defeat rebel called in his "magicians, and the astrologers, and the sorcerers, and the Chaldeans" (vs. 2). After their incompetence was clearly demonstrated by their inability to tell Nebuchadnezzar the dream and its interpretation, one might assume that he would tell them all to get out of his presence so he could call Daniel. But he did no such thing. Instead of calling Daniel, whom he himself had proven to be ten times better than all his occult confidants, Nebuchadnezzar became "angry and very furious, and commanded to destroy all the wise men of Babylon" (vs. 12), including Daniel and his three friends.

When word of this angst-filled decision came to Daniel, he asked Arioch, the king's captain, why the matter was so urgent and drastic. When Daniel found out, he approached Nebuchadnezzar and asked for time enough to get the answer. Daniel then solicited the prayers of his three friends, and in the night, God visited Daniel with both the dream and its interpretation. For such amazing answer to prayer, Daniel glorified the Lord Jehovah by ascribing the right of honor to Him and offering praise to Him. After thanking and blessing God for His intervention and help, Daniel went back to Arioch, who ushered Daniel into the king's presence.

In Nebuchadnezzar's audience, Daniel gave glory to Jehovah God again, saying, "There is a God in heaven that revealeth secrets" (vs. 28), and telling the king both his dream and the interpretation so that Nebuchadnezzar might know the thoughts of his own heart. In other words, the dream had both personal and prophetic significance. The dream was personal in that the king thought himself (the head of gold) better and more valuable than anyone else. Prophetically, the dream applied to the four main Gentile kingdoms of ancient history, with Babylon being the first, or head, of all these kingdoms.

Once Daniel had revealed both the dream and the interpretation, "Nebuchadnezzar fell upon his face, and worshipped Daniel, and commanded that they should offer an oblation and sweet odours unto him" (vs. 46). Daniel had ascribed the glory to God, but the king's concession to Daniel was aborted. Daniel's God was "a God of gods, and a Lord of kings, and a revealer of secrets" (vs. 47). By using the indefinite article, Nebuchadnezzar was admitting that Daniel's God was one of many of such caliber, but not conceding that Daniel's God was the *only* One of such a nature. To him, Jehovah God was not yet the One to be worshiped exclusively. He rewarded Daniel by promoting him and his three friends to have governing power over the affairs of Babylon.

Did Nebuchadnezzar admit defeat? Did the embarrassment of having ordered mass execution of his demonic counselors only to have this Jewish boy save the day change Nebuchadnezzar? Did he back down? No. This Babylonian king was an I-will-not-admit-defeat rebel who would deify Daniel and the false gods but would not humble himself and deify the true God.

I Will Not Admit Defeat by Enlightenment

Next in line in the biblical record of this I-will-not-admit-defeat rebel is the account of Hananiah, Mishael and Azariah in the fiery furnace in Daniel 3. This "head of gold" king was so enamored of his own importance and power that he had constructed "in the plain of Dura, in the province of Babylon" a ninety-foot-high golden statue of himself. Having invited every important person in the kingdom to the dedication of this image (for purposes of emperor worship), and having orchestrated a massive musical performance for the worship time itself, Nebuchadnezzar had a herald give the command that everyone in attendance was to bow or be thrown into the fiery furnace. Hananiah, Mishael and Azariah did not bow, and their refusal to bow was reported to Nebuchadnezzar, who asked them if the accusation was true. He then gave them one further opportunity to bow, along with a renewed, personal threat of the fiery furnace. To make his point all the more irresistible, he asked them, "Who is that God that shall deliver you out of my hands?" (vs. 15).

The answer of these three Hebrews challenges the faith of all who read it. They simply told the king that God *was* able to deliver them, that God *would* deliver them in some way, but that if his deliverance was not *from* the flames, it would be *through* them. "Then was Nebuchadnezzar full of fury, and the form of his visage was changed" (vs. 19) as he hastily commanded the furnace to be heated seven times hotter than ever before. Then, the three Hebrew young men were bound in their clothes and hurled into the furnace whose flames were so hot that they caused the death of the king's servants who threw them in. Hananiah, Mishael and Azariah "fell down bound into the midst of the burning fiery furnace" (vs. 23). They were not near the edge of this inferno; they were in the middle of it. Still, the "three men bound" became the "four men loose," and Nebuchadnezzar called them forth to be examined.

Nebuchadnezzar was given light. Scripture does not say that anyone else saw four men loose. Nebuchadnezzar said, "Lo, I see four men loose, walking in the midst of the fire, and they have no hurt; and the form of the fourth is like the Son of God" (vs. 25). After they came forth from the flames, Nebuchadnezzar examined them. Then all the guests were given opportunity to examine these three "upon whose bodies the fire had no power" (vs. 27), and Nebuchadnezzar issued an executive decree that no one in the kingdom was allowed from that day forward to "speak any thing amiss against the God of Shadrach, Meshach, and Abed-nego" (vs. 29) without risk of death and public shame.

But did Nebuchadnezzar admit defeat? Did he publicly decry the idol he had erected, commanding it to be removed? Did he require the worship of the God of the three Hebrews with the same fervency he had just moments before employed in demanding the worship of his own image? Did the light of truth and the vision of the Son of God bring him to his knees in admission of defeat? No. Nebuchadnezzar was an I-will-not-admit-defeat rebel who, even in the face of evidence that Jehovah was Almighty, even in the face of embarrassment that his own counselors were powerless and irrelevant, even in the face of enlightenment as to the true God, would not humble himself and repent toward God.

I Will Not Admit Defeat by Exhortation

In the fourth chapter of Daniel, the dreaming king had another dream. In this instance, he remembered the dream but could not interpet it. He saw a tree of great height with healthy leaves and prolific fruit and animals receiving sustenance from it while fowls rested within its foliage. In the dream, "a watcher and an holy one came down from heaven" (vs. 13) and cut down the tree, cut off its branches, shook off its leaves, scattered its fruit and chased away the animals that had benefited from it. The stump was left in the earth to be wetted with the dew for seven years. Again, King Nebuchadnezzar called in his loyal but incompetent and ineffective magicians, soothsayers and astrologers. They could not tell the meaning of this dream any more than they could declare the interpretation of the previous vision. This time, however, King Nebuchadnezzar dispensed with the death threats and just called Daniel, who came into his presence and told the king all his heart.

Daniel was immediately aware of the meaning of the dream, and its meaning so troubled him that he could not express himself for an hour. When Nebuchadnezzar assured him that he could tell the vision, Daniel said, "My lord, the dream be to them that hate thee, and the interpretation thereof to thine enemies" (vs. 19). He went on to tell that the tree was Nebuchadnezzar himself, that all the health of the tree represented the prosperity of his kingdom, and that the animals and fowls pictured the many peoples under his dictatorship. Then, Daniel told Nebuchadnezzar that the Holy Watcher was God coming to depose him, not through *military invasion* but through *divine intervention*. Specifically, God would take away his mental capacity and deliver him to animal-like existence for seven years, after which his sanity and kingdom would be restored to him.

In fearlessness, Daniel then exhorted, "Wherefore, O king, let my counsel be acceptable unto thee, and break off thy sins by righteousness, and thine iniquities by shewing mercy to the poor; if it may be a lengthening of thy tranquillity" (vs. 27). Did this exhortation stop the king in his tracks? Did he plead with Daniel, asking him how he could avoid such a fate? Did the king fall on his face and cry out in despair to God? No. He was an I-will-not-admit-defeat rebel who thought he could overcome this situation. One year later, Nebuchadnezzar's day of grace was up. He crossed the line between God's mercy and His wrath as he blithely "walked in the palace of the kingdom of Babylon....and said, Is not this great Babylon, that I have built...by the might of my power, and for the honour of my majesty?" (vss. 29, 30). The fulfillment of the dream fell at that moment upon him.

The beautiful ending of this I-will-not-admit-defeat rebel's life is that upon his admission of defeat at the close of the seven years, God restored both his sanity and his kingdom. He humbled himself before the one true God whose evidence, embarrassment, enlightenment and exhortation he had before so stubbornly spurned. In personal testimony, this former I-will-not-admit-defeat rebel stated,

"At the end of the days I Nebuchadnezzar lifted up mine eyes unto heaven, and mine understanding returned unto me, and I blessed the most High, and I praised and honoured him that liveth for ever, whose dominion is an everlasting dominion, and his kingdom is from generation to generation.

"Now I Nebuchadnezzar praise and extol and honour the King of heaven, all whose works are truth, and his ways judgment: and those that walk in pride he is able to abase."—Vss. 34, 37.

Here is one I-will-not-admit-defeat rebel who admitted defeat, and we will see him when we come from the east and the west and sit down with Abraham, Isaac and Jacob in the kingdom of God!

Haman, the Son of Hammedatha the Agagite

God's sovereignty and majesty are seldom seen in the fashion so dramatically and beautifully given in the restoration Book of Esther. The Jews were back from their Babylonian captivity, the temple was built, and the Medo-Persian Ahasuerus in Shushan had decided to make a gala feast to show off his riches and honor to all the princes and prime ministers from each of his one hundred twenty-seven provinces. During the course of the festivities, he called his wife Vashti to a public display of her beauty, but Vashti refused. Due to her refusal, she was rejected as queen, and the search for a replacement began.

Esther, an orphan and a descendant of captive Jews, had been cared for in childhood by her cousin Mordecai in Shushan. Esther was obedient to her cousin as if Mordecai had actually been her father, and when Esther was selected as a possible candidate to be the new queen, she obtained favor of all who saw her. Ahasuerus chose her, and "he set the royal crown upon her head, and made her queen instead of Vashti" (Esther 2:17). Interestingly, all this was done without anyone in Shushan the palace knowing that she was a Jew, because

"Esther had not yet shewed her kindred nor her people; as Mordecai had charged her: for Esther did the commandment of Mordecai, like as when she was brought up with him" (vs. 20).

In those early days when Esther was on the throne and her cousin Mordecai was sitting in the king's gate, there came knowledge to Mordecai of a plot against the life of Ahasuerus. Mordecai revealed the plot of Bigthan and Teresh, two of the king's doorkeepers, to Esther, who relayed this information to her husband the king, and the disloyal courtiers were hanged. Oddly enough, Ahasuerus did not promote Mordecai or do him any honor for his fidelity. Instead, Ahasuerus promoted Haman, the son of Hammedatha, an Agagite, to be above all the other provincial princes (prime ministers) in the realm.

I-Will-Not-Admit-Defeat Pettiness

One of the perks of the position occupied by Haman was that the king commanded all the subjects of the kingdom to bow to him. Haman loved all that attention, and as he walked along the streets of Shushan, through the gates to the king's palace, and within the courtyards of the palace itself, the loyal subjects bowed and made much ado over this pompous, self-inflated, egotistical, I-will-not-admit-defeat rebel—all the loyal subjects but one, that is. Mordecai would not bow. Like Hananiah, Mishael and Azariah before him, he would not bow. Most likely, he obtained courage from those storied youths, and he determined he was not going to bow his head to an enemy of the people of God. This isolated, nonbowing Jew troubled the petty Haman. Hundreds of people bowed on any given public occasion as Haman executed the state affairs of his exalted office, yet he was so perturbed by the one who did not bow that all those who did bow were esteemed as nothing.

I-Will-Not-Admit-Defeat Prevarication

In a rage because of this thing, Haman "thought scorn to

lay hands on Mordecai alone; for they had shewed him the people of Mordecai: wherefore Haman sought to destroy all the Jews that were throughout the whole kingdom of Ahasuerus" (3:6). Haman made no delay in procuring the king's favor to wipe out the Jews. He represented the Jews as a "certain people scattered abroad and dispersed among the people in all the provinces of thy kingdom," as having laws that were "diverse from all people" (vs. 8). This much was true, but to avoid the possibility of defeat, he prevaricated on two points: these people were both lawless and unprofitable to the king and kingdom. Without revealing who these people were, and without detailing the magnitude of the slaughter that would take place, Haman convinced Ahasuerus that it would be profitable to have the entire group slain. The way Haman presented this matter to the king made it seem as if this were an insignificant number of rabble-rousing riffraff who needed to be expunged. The king authorized the financing of this project out of the king's treasury, and he and Haman—the Old Testament Hitler—determined by the casting of lots the day for the actual genocide.

News of this pending doom of the Jews reached Mordecai in the gate, and he went into a fast with rending of clothes, sackcloth and ashes and public mourning. Mordecai's lamentation was copied in every province where Haman's edict was posted. Queen Esther's maids got wind of the matter and reported it to her as a matter of palace news. Esther called Hatach, one of the king's chamberlains, to approach Mordecai and ask him for details. Mordecai told Hatach about the decree and the money promised to finance it. Then he gave Hatach a copy of the writing and sent a message for Esther to approach Ahasuerus to plead for her people. At first, Esther declined because the king had not summoned her for thirty days and because no one could go unsummoned to the king without threat of death. Mordecai sent word again, saying that if she did not plead for her people, she would be slain with them. He further encouraged her with his opinion that God had apparently raised her up in the kingdom for just such a desperate situation.

Resolving to make intercession, Esther first commanded that Mordecai and all the Jews in Shushan fast and pray for her; she and her maidens did likewise. She then approached Ahasuerus and invited him and Haman to a dinner where she would tell the king her request. Haman was thrilled to have been invited to a banquet with no other guests but the king and queen! He and the king attended the banquet, but Esther hid her purpose and invited Haman and the king to another banquet of identical nature the next day.

I-Will-Not-Admit-Defeat Pontification

On the way home from this first banquet, he passed Mordecai, who did not bow; but he refrained from expressing indignation and hurried home to Zeresh, his wife, where his I-will-not-admit-defeat rebellion came to the surface. He called together his friends and family to pontificate on the *prize* of all his riches, of all his *privileges* in Shushan the palace, and of his *private invitation* to a second banquet with the king and queen. But even this pretentious, self-exalting bombast did not satiate his ego, for he said, "Yet all this availeth me nothing, so long as I see Mordecai the Jew sitting at the king's gate" (5:13). When Haman's wife heard this, she suggested construction of a seventy-five-foot-high gallows on which to hang Mordecai the very next day.

Whether it was the noise of the construction of this massive gallows or a divine visitation, the king could not sleep that night. He asked for a reader to read the court chronicles to him in hopes that the boring accounts might lull him to sleep. As the reader pored through the minutiae of executive actions and decrees, he came upon the account of Mordecai's informing the king of the two who conspired to take his life. As the reader passed over that event, the king interrupted him and asked what honor had been given to Mordecai for his integrity. The reader carefully perused the account again and, seeing no record of any action, said, "There is nothing done for him" (6:3).

At that moment, the king heard hasty footsteps on the courtyard's marble floors and asked the reader who was walking there. The reader stood up and looked out into the court so he could see and told the king it was Haman. Haman was preparing to approach the king for permission to hang Mordecai, probably having just come from an inspection of the gallows. The king summoned Haman to his presence in the royal bedchamber.

I-Will-Not-Admit-Defeat Presumption

Haman jumped at this chance for such private, personal proximity to Ahasuerus and came right in. The king asked him what should be done for someone whom the king delighted to honor. Haman's I-will-not-admit-defeat rebellion oozed forth again. In his ostentatious, overrated view of himself, he presumed there would be no one whom the king would delight to honor above him. With his rebellious hope on the throne itself and with his rebellious eye envisioning himself receiving such honors, he presumptuously suggested that the person whom the king delighted to honor be paraded through the streets wearing the king's crown and apparel and riding on the king's horse, while a herald cried out, "Thus shall it be done to the man whom the king delighteth to honour" (vs. 9). Imagine Haman's horror when the king popped his rebellious, I-will-not-admit-defeat bubble by telling him to do just that for Mordecai and to be the herald who announced Mordecai's honors!

When Haman completed his day-long, humiliating parade

through the streets of Shushan proclaiming the honorable virtues of Mordecai, he "hasted to his house mourning, and having his head covered" (vs. 12). After he told his wife and friends what had happened, Zeresh warned him, "If Mordecai be of the seed of the Jews, before whom thou hast begun to fall, thou shalt not prevail against him, but shalt surely fall before him" (vs. 13). Just as God gave Pilate warning and opportunity for repentance through his wife five centuries later (Matt. 27:19), God allowed Haman this little window of time to repent, for even as his wife spoke, the king's chamberlains arrived to transport Haman to Esther's second private banquet. God, in that moment, gave the I-will-not-admit-defeat rebel Haman a chance to give in.

I-Will-Not-Admit-Defeat Pretense

As that second banquet got under way, the king asked Esther her request. She boldly petitioned the king for her own life and for the lives of her people who had been slated for utter destruction, even though that very destruction would bring damage to the king. With incredulous surprise, the king asked who would hatch such a plot and where this enemy might be. In answer to this question, Esther pointed the finger and said, "The adversary and enemy is this wicked Haman" (7:6).

Haman certainly knew the power and wrath of an upset Ahasuerus! Could he at that moment have pleaded for mercy? He could have, but because he was an I-will-not-admit-defeat rebel, he would not. Instead of following the king to the palace garden to plead for his life, he fell across the queen's bed in an insincere pretense of sorrow aimed at convincing the queen he deserved a reprieve. When the king returned from his pacings to and fro and saw Haman on the queen's bed, he exploded. Harbonah, one of his chamberlains, suggested that the gallows that Haman had prepared for Mordecai might be suitable for Haman instead. The king commanded it to be so, and it was, and the king was appeased. The petty, prevaricating rebel had pontificated to his family, presumed upon the king and pretended in the presence of the queen. His demise could have been averted by a simple admission, but then, I-will-not-admit-defeat rebels don't do that.

Haman's I-will-not-admit-defeat rebellion was uncovered in a matter of days and returned upon his own head in a matter of moments. In the case of Pharaoh, weeks elapsed between Moses' first encounter with him and his drowning in the Red Sea. For Nebuchadnezzar, decades came and went while he hasted headlong toward almost sure dishonor, which he narrowly evaded. Regardless of the chronology and outcome, the stubbornness and resolve of rebels who live by the I-will-not-admit-defeat rule is immense.

Illustration

A young wife became a believer after having been married for about seven years. Her husband remained unconverted. As her life became conformed to Christ, her husband retreated into a defensive mode that turned him into a modern-day Nabal who fought every step of faith and obedience she attempted to take. In a move of vengeance, he began an affair; and after only about two months, his wife discovered it all. The husband would not, however, admit defeat. Instead, he left and moved three states away. This Christian lady continued to be faithful to God and followed her pastor's counsel to invite her husband to return to her but not to go to him in his sin. She regularly called and periodically sent letters expressing her forgiveness, her longing to have him back and her willingness to take him back.

After about six years, news reached this lady that her husband was dying of AIDS in a hospital in the city where he had moved. With a trusted friend and her pastor's wife, she went to the town and found him. His first words to her were, "I'm not defeated, Woman! I'll lick this!" He died three weeks later, and, according to his nurse, some of his last words were that he would never admit to his wife that her way was the right way.

The Rule That the Righteous Live By

Humility

If rebels live by the pride of refusing to admit defeat, it stands to reason that Christians ought to admit defeat readily when they are wrong or misguided. Such admission is nothing more than simple humility. Scripture says much of this precious commodity of the Christian soul. Each one is to be "clothed with humility" (I Pet. 5:5), a statement that literally means that the believer is to be wrapped about as if with an apron symbolizing servitude. The prophet Micah boldly told Israel, "Walk humbly with thy God" (6:8), informing the believer that this is one of God's requirements. The holy and beloved "elect of God" are commanded to "put on...humbleness of mind" (Col. 3:12). This command is repeated in I Peter 5:6, where the apostle tells believers, "Humble yourselves therefore under the mighty hand of God," and in James 4:10, where it says, "Humble yourselves in the sight of the Lord."

While there are multiplied negatives associated with I-will-not-admit-defeat rebellion, there are multiplied positives affiliated with humility. Both Proverbs 15:33 and 18:12 tells us, "Before honour is humility." Humility is the avenue toward the honor that the I-will-not-admit-defeat rebel erroneously believes he can achieve by his arrogance. Again, James 4:6 and I Peter 5:5 both tell us that, in addition to the uplifting that follows humility, God gives grace to those who humble themselves. Matthew 23:12 also says, "He that shall humble himself shall be exalted." Truly profitable service to the Lord must be done with "all humility of mind" (Acts 20:19). In the matter of prayer, God "forgetteth not the cry of the humble" (Ps. 9:12).

Proverbs 16:19 declares that a "humble spirit" is better in value than great riches. Perhaps the greatest advantage of all to humility is found in Isaiah 57:15, where God avers that he "dwell[s] in the high and holy place, with him also that is of a contrite and humble spirit, to revive the spirit of the humble, and to revive the heart of the contrite ones."

Pharaoh, Nebuchadnezzar and Haman could all three have immensely benefited from humility. Recalcitrant refusal to admit defeat destroyed Pharaoh, his nation and his army. This same poisonous potion destroyed Haman and confined him to the gallows on earth and the flames in eternity. And were it not for the constant prayers and witness of Daniel, I-will-not-admit-defeat rebellion might well have destroyed Nebuchadnezzar as well. Any person who would rid himself of I-will-not-admit-defeat rebellion must get off his high horse and get down very low. He must sincerely and honestly acknowledge his smallness and insignificance to God. He must repent of an arrogance that brings defeat and start all over. He would do well to "remember all the way which the LORD [his] God led [him]…to humble [him]" (Deut. 8:2), so he can have a fresh beginning with God.

9
The They-Can-Why-Can't-I Rule

"When thou art bidden of any man to a wedding, sit not down in the highest room; lest a more honourable man than thou be bidden of him;

"And he that bade thee and him come and say to thee, Give this man place; and thou begin with shame to take the lowest room.

"But when thou art bidden, go and sit down in the lowest room; that when he that bade thee cometh, he may say unto thee, Friend, go up higher: then shalt thou have worship in the presence of them that sit at meat with thee."—Luke 14:8–10.

"Let every man abide in the same calling wherein he was called.

"Art thou called being a servant? care not for it: but if thou mayest be made free, use it rather.

"For he that is called in the Lord, being a servant, is the Lord's freeman: likewise also he that is called, being free, is Christ's servant.

"Ye are bought with a price; be not ye the servants of men.

"Brethren, let every man, wherein he is called, therein abide with God."—I Cor. 7:20–24.

"And no man taketh this honour unto himself, but he that is called of God, as was Aaron.

"So also Christ glorified not himself to be made an high priest;

*but he that said unto him, Thou art my Son, to day have I begot-
ten thee."*—Heb. 5:4, 5.

This chapter and chapter 11 of this book are closely related.
This chapter is dedicated to rebels who believe they should be
able to do anything that anyone else is called, equipped and
authorized to do. Chapter 11 deals with the attitude that those
who are called, equipped and authorized by God have really
only exalted themselves over other believers.

The rebel who keeps the they-can-why-can't-I rule sees his
own merits as elevating him to the level of one who, having
been saved, has been "called…with an holy calling, not according to [his] works, but according to [God's] own purpose and
grace" (II Tim. 1:9). This type of rebel becomes disgruntled
with what he perceives to be limitations within his own calling.
Instead of faithfully pursuing God's unique and fruitful leading for his own life, he despises his own calling and covets the
calling and labor God assigned to someone else.

Nadab and Abihu

Nadab and Abihu are among the they-can-why-can't-I
rebels of God's Word. The first eight chapters of Leviticus
record in specific details the offerings, the laws of the offerings, the laws governing the high priest, and the laws of the
general priesthood called after the order of Aaron. Chapter 9
shows the beginning of the carrying out of these laws. Aaron,
the high priest, offered for himself and for the people. The
priests brought the blood to Aaron, and he applied it. They
brought him the entrails, and he burnt them on the altar. He
waved the breasts and right shoulder of the peace offering.

After all the work was done, Aaron raised his hand and
blessed the people and then came down from offering the sin
offering, the burnt offering and the peace offerings. At the
end of chapter 9, when all the instructions had been given and

the offerings had been properly prepared, "the glory of the LORD appeared unto all the people. And there came a fire out from before the LORD, and consumed upon the altar the burnt-offering and the fat: which when all the people saw, they shouted, and fell on their faces" (Leviticus 9:23, 24). The first two verses of chapter 10 record three facets of they-can-why-can't-I rebellion as illustrated in the experience of Nadab and Abihu, two of Aaron's four sons.

They-Can-Why-Can't-I Intrusion

Obviously these two elder sons of Aaron intruded into territory not given to them. Nadab and Abihu rebelliously concluded that since Aaron had gone into the tabernacle of the congregation, they could too. After all, they were priests. They were even better than priests; they were sons of the high priest! Priests go into the tabernacle and present offerings. Their entrance into the tabernacle to offer upon the altar of incense was a step into territory reserved for Aaron, but in their they-can-why-can't-I rebellion, they moved without reservation or hesitation.

They-Can-Why-Can't-I Presumption

They-can-why-can't-I rebellion is presumptuous in motive. In similar fashion to His manifestation at the completion of the tabernacle in Exodus 40:34, the Lord had just appeared in direct fulfillment of His promise to Aaron in Leviticus 9:4 and 6. The fire, representative of God's presence among His people and of His approval of their offering, lit the fire of the altar that the priests were then to maintain continually so that the fire would "never go out" (Lev. 6:12, 13).

The presumption is seen in the fact that, although incense had been burned on the altar when it was set up in Exodus 40:27, God had given no instruction yet regarding the manner in which the fire on the incense altar was to be kindled.

First, their presumption was against God personally as they presumed to know how to light the fire on the altar of incense when God had not spoken. This brings out a key that is part of they-can-why-can't-I rebellion. These rebels do not wait for God to speak. Leviticus 10:1 calls their deed "strange fire...which he commanded them not," indicating that God had given no word about this; nor does God speak instructively regarding worship to rebels of any type. They-can-why-can't-I rebels rush ahead to do what they decide to do, and their presumption is made all the more lawless and reprehensible because they often pursue a religious-looking path of action.

Then, Nadab and Abihu were presumptuous against God in the practical realm as well, assuming that the fire on the altar of incense was to be lit in similar fashion to the lighting of the fire upon the altar of offerings. This facet of their presumption relegated God to the realm of boring predictability and deprived Him of His infinite originality and diversity. Truly, God is predictable in matters bound by His own faithfulness and steadfastness, but He is not ever predictable in the arena of man's reasoning.

They-Can-Why-Can't-I Conclusion

Like all rebels, they-can-why-can't-I rebels draw inaccurate and, in this case, disastrous conclusions. These two priestly sons of Aaron concluded, albeit without any divine authority, that their offering was just as sanctified as Aaron's offering, that their "strange fire" was just as acceptable as God's holy fire, and that their "will worship" was just as right as the worship that was according to God's revelation. What they discovered too late is that what is done in presumptuous rebellion is never the same as what is done in prostrate reverence.

Twenty-first century saints, whose culture has been steeped in relativism and compromise for at least the last six decades, may find this portion of Scripture intolerant and harsh. It may even appear to some that God was unduly rash, but the truth is that Nadab and Abihu rebelled against the Lord by intruding where they did not belong, by presuming what God had given no reason to presume and by concluding something based upon false premises.

King Saul

In outlining his esteemed Scofield Study Bible, C. I. Scofield entitled the thirteenth chapter of I Samuel "The self-will of Saul." It would be difficult to imagine a more accurate title. Saul's unknown, humble beginnings and his littleness in his own sight (I Sam. 15:17) quickly gave way to an arrogance that was his unnecessary destruction in the early years of his kingship, his utter destruction in the middle years and his *ultimate* destruction in the later years.

As to the reign of Saul, God tolerated but never authorized it. When Israel demanded a king (8:5), Samuel lamented, but the Lord told him to let the people have their way because they had not rejected Samuel, but God Himself.

God then spoke to Samuel on a given day and said, "To morrow about this time I will send thee a man out of the land of Benjamin, and thou shalt anoint him to be captain over my people Israel...for I have looked upon my people, because their cry is come unto me" (9:16). In other words, God, having observed the dissatisfied, disgruntled heart of His people and having heard their murmuring, grumbling cry, chose a man who would be what they deserved.

Saul, out searching for his father's donkeys that had gone astray, encountered Samuel in a particular city the next day, "and when Samuel saw Saul, the LORD said unto him, Behold the man whom I spake to thee of!" (vs. 17). Samuel and Saul ate together that day, and the next morning Samuel anointed him as king over Israel.

On that occasion, Samuel gave Saul three confirmatory signs that the Lord had elevated him to be king. First, Samuel told Saul that he and his servant would encounter that day at Rachel's sepulcher near Zelzah two men who would tell them that the donkeys which they were seeking had been found, and that Saul's father was now concerned for his son's safety. Next, Samuel told Saul and his servant to expect to meet three men near Tabor who would be carrying three kids, three loaves of bread and a wine bottle respectively. Samuel told Saul that these men would greet him and give him two loaves of bread. Third, Saul and his servant would meet a company of the prophets near the hill of God, and the Spirit of God would come upon Saul, and he would prophesy and "be turned into another man" (10:6).

Then Samuel gave Saul one instruction to follow. He told Saul to do as the Lord bid him and then go down to Gilgal. At Gilgal, he was to wait seven days until Samuel came to him there "to offer burnt-offerings, and to sacrifice sacrifices of peace-offerings" (vs. 8). At that point, Samuel would show Saul what Saul was supposed to do next—simple enough; simple, that is, for anyone but a they-can-why-can't-I rebel.

The rest of chapter ten is devoted to the actual choosing by lot and coronation of King Saul. Chapter 11 deals with Saul's victory over the Ammonites at Jabesh-gilead, and that chapter ends with Samuel encouraging the people to go to Gilgal to renew the kingdom there. In the next chapter, Samuel gave the people a brief history of their nation over whom the Lord had reigned, explained the gravity of their sin in insisting that God give them a king, but then reassured them that even though they had sinned greatly, they could serve God from then on. Samuel even assured them of his continual prayers for them.

In chapter 13, just two years into the reign of Saul, his downfall began with a breach of trust with regard to the one single command Samuel had given him on the day of his anointing. Like Adam and Eve before him, it was not the multiplicity of rules that caused him to rebel but the fact that he was recalcitrant and unruly.

Once Saul's son Jonathan had smitten one of the Philistine garrisons, the Philistines hated the Hebrews more than before. They gathered their forces to Michmash, and Saul rallied his men at Gilgal. The Philistines outnumbered Israel, and Israel was already distressed, afraid and trembling. The Israelite army was scattered from Saul, so "Saul said, Bring hither a burnt-offering to me, and peace-offerings. And he offered the burnt-offering" (vs. 9). Just as soon as Saul had offered that burnt-offering, Samuel appeared on the scene, "and Samuel said, What hast thou done?" (vs. 11).

Saul, in keeping with they-can-why-can't-I rebellion, demonstrated the same intrusion, presumption and conclusion that Nadab and Abihu had shown. However, Saul was not consumed in an instant for his rebellion, probably because he was in Gilgal, not in the Tabernacle. This gave Saul an opportunity for the lame exercise of explaining to Samuel the excuses for his they-can-why-can't-I rebellion, which Nadab and Abihu would no doubt have also attempted had they survived long enough to do so!

They-Can-Why-Can't-I Trepidation

Five times in I Samuel 13, the Scripture mentions words and phrases associated with fear: "in a strait," "distressed," "hide themselves," "trembling" and "scattered" (vss. 6–8). When he began his paltry explanation for intrusion into Samuel's duties, he cited the fact that the people were scattered from him; that is, they were in disarray and confusion (vs. 11). In other words, the people were following their fearful, confused leader. Saul was a man of fright and fear, but his fear was the fear of man which "bringeth a snare" (Prov. 29:25), not the fear of God which would have made him a man of faith and fortitude. Had Saul developed the fear of God, he would never have engaged in intrusion and presumption, but because he was paralyzed by trepidation among men, he succumbed quickly to grave sin. They-can-why-can't-I rebellion creates insecurity because the rebel knows deep inside that he is out of place.

Likewise, it seems that Nadab and Abihu feared man, because they waited for Aaron to come out of the Tabernacle before they went in, knowing that Aaron would have disapproved and driven them from that holy place. Had they feared God, not man, their story would have had an opposite outcome. This reveals that the whole outlook of a they-can-why-can't-I rebel is devoid of the fear of the Lord. Those who choose not *to fear God with reverence* are doomed *to fear man with regrets.*

They-Can-Why-Can't-I Accusation

Samuel told Saul on the day of his anointing, "And thou shalt go down before me to Gilgal...seven days shalt thou tarry, till I come to thee, and shew thee what thou shalt do" (I Sam. 10:8). Saul did tarry "seven days, according to the set time that Samuel had appointed" (13:8), but then he straightway intruded into the priestly duties of offering the sacrifice. No sooner had he done so than Samuel appeared. That means that Samuel could not have been more than a mile outside the camp when Saul began his offering!

When Samuel arrived, Saul told him, "Thou camest not within the days appointed" (vs. 11). This statement would be funny if it were not so absurd! How could Saul have been talking to Samuel on the seventh day if Samuel had not come on the seventh day in the time appointed? When a they-can-why-can't-I rebel has presumed to intrude where he does not belong, it is common for him to seek to justify himself by accusing others.

They-Can-Why-Can't-I Procrastination

The next part of Saul's report to Samuel in verse 12 mentions that he had "not made supplication unto the LORD." The delay of Samuel for seven days was in accord with God's plan and Samuel's prophecy on the day Saul was anointed. Saul's procrastintion in prayer was not in accord with God's plan and had nothing to do with the issue! There was no limit on Saul's prayers—when he prayed or how long he prayed. The limitation placed on Saul was that Samuel would come and offer the sacrifices and offerings. Interestingly, Saul did *not* offer prayers which he should have offered, but he *did* offer a sacrifice which he should not have offered. How differently this might have turned out had Saul realized his need for prayer and begun praying so that upon Samuel's arrival, Saul would have been found *prostrated in prayer*, not procrastinating in prayer. How diametrically opposite this might have been if Saul had *delayed his intrusion and delved into intercession!*

They-Can-Why-Can't-I Admission

When Saul concluded his explanation to Samuel, he said, "I forced myself therefore, and offered a burnt-offering (vs. 12)." This was spoken almost as a disclaimer. It was as if Saul were saying he had been placed into a situation where he had no choice. In short, he was admitting that he had intruded and presumed upon God, but he was claiming that God would have to overlook the transgression because Samuel, not to say God Himself, had left him no option. They-can-why-can't-I rebels—indeed all rebels—often resort to this type of admission that is no admission at all.

They-Can-Why-Can't-I Disqualification

Sadly, Saul's intrusion, presumption and conclusion which he attempted to justify by means of his trepidation, accusation, procrastination and admission brought about his disqualification. Samuel told him,

> "*Thou hast done foolishly: thou hast not kept the commandment of the* LORD *thy God, which he commanded thee: for now would the* LORD *have established thy kingdom upon Israel for ever.*
>
> "*But now thy kingdom shall not continue...because thou hast not kept that which the* LORD *commanded thee.*"—Vss. 13,14.

This divine pronouncement of displeasure occurred within the first two years of Saul's forty-year reign. For thirty-eight more years, he ruled with this sword of Damocles over his head, all because of intrusion into where he did not belong, presumption of what was not his, and conclusions that were based on the twisted understanding of they-can-why-can't-I rebellion.

Incidentally, it is not until I Samuel 14:35, after Samuel's grim pronouncement of the discontinuance of Saul's kingdom, that God says of Saul, "And Saul built an altar unto the LORD: the same was the first altar that he built unto the LORD." Had he built his altars to Jehovah God first, he might have circumvented many personal troubles and somewhat averted the tragic failure of his kingdom, or perhaps even avoided that demise altogether.

King Uzziah

When Uzziah (also called Azariah) ascended the throne of Judah at age sixteen, he inherited leadership of a nation that had just recently been ravaged by war between his father Amaziah and King Joash of the ten northern tribes of Israel. Uzziah's fifty-two-year reign was the second longest in the history of the southern kingdom of Judah, exceeded only by Manasseh's fifty-five years in power. King Uzziah 'did right in God's sight' and "sought God in the days of Zechariah, who had understanding in the visions of God: and as long as he sought the LORD, God made him to prosper" (II Chron. 26:4, 5).

That statement from the chronicler shows that Uzziah was not a haphazard king with no aim or focus. To the contrary, Uzziah was possibly the most industrious and prodigious king Judah ever had. The human author catalogued a long list of Uzziah's outstanding accomplishments. He defeated the Philistines, Judah's perpetual enemies. He achieved fame and the respect of many pagan nations. He rebuilt the gates and towers and the city wall of Jerusalem that had been knocked down after his father's ill-fated war against King Joash of Israel. He put lookout towers in the desert, dug wells for the cattle and promoted agriculture in all the fertile places of his kingdom. He developed a formidable army great in number, skill and weaponry. He even oversaw the invention of new defense mechanisms that would shoot arrows and great stones from the towers and walls in the event of an invasion.

They-Can-Why-Can't-I Deception

The grand statement about Uzziah—that as long as he focused on God, God blessed and prospered him—is followed by this catalogue of achievements. Sadly, the achieving of a large number of ambitious goals deceived King Uzziah. What follows is a grievous statement of King Uzziah's they-can-why-can't-I rebellion: "When he was strong, his heart was lifted up to his destruction: for he transgressed against the LORD his God, and went into the temple of the LORD to burn incense upon the altar of incense" (vs. 16). He was deceived, as are all rebels, into thinking he would not fall.

At that time, God's appointed high priest was a faithful and loyal man named Azariah. This Azariah, along with "fourscore priests of the LORD, that were valiant men…withstood Uzziah the king, and said unto him, It appertaineth not unto thee, Uzziah, to burn incense unto the LORD" (vss. 17, 18). These godly men then ordered the king out of the sanctuary, but

Uzziah responded in anger. At that moment, God smote him with leprosy.

Whether Uzziah realized his leprosy first or whether Azariah and the priests saw it first is not revealed, but suffice it to say they all realized what had occurred, and the priests "thrust him out from thence; yea, himself hasted also to go out, because the LORD had smitten him" (vs. 20). From that day forward, Uzziah was a leper who lived separate from others, while his son Jotham was co-regent in leadership of the nation.

The same intrusion that Nadab, Abihu and King Saul exhibited was evident in King Uzziah. The priests told Uzziah that the offering of incense did not pertain to him; that is, it was not his job, his calling, his place. Again, what Nadab, Abihu and King Saul demonstrated in the realm of presumption was evident in King Uzziah's angry response to priestly rebuke. King Uzziah also showed that he had drawn rebellious conclusions when he allowed his own heart to be lifted up. Whether they die instantly like Nadab and Abihu, reign tragically like Saul or live separated from others by leprosy like Uzziah, all they-can-why-can't-I rebels live by these three aspects of rebellion against the Lord, and they all reap in some fashion what is commensurate with their insistance that they be able to lift themselves up to a place God never gave them. How different and how much better would their lives be if they would simply abide in the calling wherein they were called!

Illustration

A factory crew chief concluded (the conclusion) that since his shop foreman did not handle a co-worker's disciplinary problem in keeping with company policy, it was his duty to step into his foreman's shoes. Going over his foreman's head (the intrusion), he approached the general manager and told the general manager that he was in error for not requiring the shop foreman to keep company policy and for not enforcing said company policy himself (the presumption). With this rebuke from an underling still hanging in the air, the general manager gave the crew chief two things. One was a logical explanation of extenuating circumstances in the co-worker's life that allowed the shop foreman to bypass the company's disciplinary policy. The other was a brusque statement: "You're fired!"

The Rule That the Righteous Live By

Contentment with Position

They-can-why-can't-I rebels find the solution to their rebellion in the development of contentment. This is not the lazy contentment that is satisfied to do little or nothing, but the spiritual contentment of which Paul spoke to Timothy when he said, "Godliness with contentment is great gain" (I Tim. 6:6). While those words specifically apply to contentment with one's possessions (see chapter 14), the truth remains that the combination of godliness and contentment brings enormous gain to those who possess it. Had the priests Nadab and Abihu and the kings Saul and Uzziah possessed godliness with contentment, not one of them would ever have coveted that position which was someone else's by calling, qualification and anointing.

The righteous believer lives by the rule of contentment with position. Rather than murmuring because someone is higher than he in work and calling, he rejoices that God has lifted him as high as He has, knowing he deserved not to be lifted at all. The ultimate lifting up is the lifting up of salvation wherein God lifts the sinner from the reach of the tongues of Hell's tormenting flames. Of the believing children of God, one reads that God "hath quickened us together with Christ...And hath raised us up together, and made us sit together in heavenly places in Christ Jesus" (Eph. 2:5, 6). Any spiritually minded, righteous child of God would be thrilled if that were the only position he was ever allowed to occupy. If all that God ever gave to anyone was the position of saved sinner, that would be far more than enough.

However, righteous believers have many more positions, far too numerous to expound upon in this short space. The righteous believer who lives by the rule of contentment with position is a servant, having the luxurious privilege of being a servant "of Christ, doing the will of God from the heart; With good will doing service, as to the Lord, and not to men" (6:6, 7).

Beyond being a servant, the righteous believer who lives by the rule of contentment with position is "no more a servant, but a son; and if a son, then an heir of God through Christ" (Gal. 4:7). The apostle John exclaims, "Behold, what manner of love the Father hath bestowed upon us, that we should be called the sons of God" (I John 3:1); and Paul informs the righteous believer that "as many as are led by the Spirit of God, they are the sons of God. For…ye have received the Spirit of adoption, whereby we cry, Abba, Father" (Rom. 8:14,15).

John introduces yet another position of the righteous believer, that of friend. The position of friend of God, friend of Christ, is such an amazing possession that one can barely comprehend it. Jesus said, "Henceforth I call you not servants; for the servant knoweth not what his lord doeth: but I have called you friends; for all things that I have heard of my Father I have made known unto you" (John 15:15). The Book of Hebrews adds to this list another position of the righteous believers when we are informed that "he [Jesus] is not ashamed to call them brethren" (Heb. 2:11).

If one were to alliterate this, he could say that the righteous child of God is *servant, son, soul mate* and *sibling* to the Lord. These positions are not to be sneezed at or deemed as nothing.

These are the spiritual privileges of those who choose to live by the rules of the righteous. God will not call a they-can-why-can't-I rebel a servant, because he is not serving but striving. Such a rebel is not living like a son, because he is not "led by the Spirit" of God (Rom. 8:14) but by "the spirit of error" (I John 4:6), the "spirit of antichrist" (vs. 3), and "the spirit of the world" (I Cor. 2:12). Our Saviour will not refer to such a rebel as a friend or soul mate because he does not do what the Lord tells him to do (John 15:14). The rebel of this chapter is not fulfilling the role of a brother, because he shames the Lord and Saviour.

The righteous choose to abide by the rule of contentment with their position. Above and beyond being the Father's son and the Saviour's servant, soul mate and sibling, that righteous one is blessed with magnificent opportunities whereby the Lord shines through his life. All of Christian living is privilege and gift and blessing to the grateful, contented child of God. He sees his position as the best place he could ever have been given; indeed, he cries out,

> "The LORD is the portion of mine inheritance and of my cup: thou maintainest my lot.
>
> "The lines are fallen unto me in pleasant places; yea, I have a goodly heritage."—Ps. 16:5, 6.

10
The Twist-History Rule

"An ungodly man diggeth up evil: and in his lips there is as a burning fire."

"Remove not the ancient landmark, which thy fathers have set."—Prov. 16:27; 22:28.

Twist-history rebels specialize in misrepresenting what actually occurred in the past as a justification for their actions in the present. The history of any people is dogged by illustrations of just such falsity. Twist-history rebels are more likely to bend personal issues than national ones, but regardless of the scope of the history, they do not tell it like it *was* and therefore do not respond to it like it *is*.

The Ten Spies

If ever history got twisted, it was in the story in Numbers 13 of the twelve spies who went to search the land of Canaan. The entire scenario is rehearsed in Deuteronomy, where Moses quite strongly indicates that the search of the land was not God's original intention but something on which the people insisted. Moses recounted the chronology of the events in Deuteronomy 1:20–22:

"And I said unto you, Ye are come unto the mountain of the Amorites, which the LORD our God doth give unto us.

> *"Behold, the* LORD *thy God hath set the land before thee: go up and possess it, as the* LORD *God of thy fathers hath said unto thee; fear not, neither be discouraged.*
>
> *"And ye came near unto me every one of you, and said, We will send men before us, and they shall search us out the land, and bring us word again by what way we must go up, and into what cities we shall come."*

Very clearly, Moses told the Exodus generation they had come to the land God had given them and they were to go up and possess it without fear or lack of courage. It was to have been a *faith* endeavor, but the people came to Moses and presented their *sight* endeavor. They wanted to search the land and see it and find out about it. God told them to possess first and *ponder* later. They decided they were more intelligent than God and that they should ponder first and possess if they could.

When Deuteronomy 1:23 says that the people's saying pleased him well, I believe that Moses was merely accommodating their carnality, much like Samuel condescended to Israel's demand for a king. Notice that when Moses instructed the twelve spies as to their duties in Numbers 13:17–20, He said four times that they were to spy out the "land" and see what it was. Along with spying on the people and sizing up the cities, they were to be searching the land. It was a land of *promise*. It was a land of *provision*. It was a land of *protection*. They were to focus on the land.

Numbers 13:27 agrees in content with Deuteronomy 1:25. The land most certainly flowed with milk and honey as God had said. The fruit of the land was such that a cluster of grapes had to be carried by two men on a pole. It truly was a good land. Unfortunately, the "nevertheless" of Numbers 13:28 and the "notwithstanding" of Deuteronomy 1:26 also agree in content. And it was after the "nevertheless" and the "notwithstanding" that history got twisted. The twist-history rebels began to turn the good report on its head, and by Numbers 13:32, "they brought up an evil report of the land which they had searched." This twisted history was not old history from centuries or generations before; rather, this twisted history was merely hours or days old. Even so, the words of the faithful minority of Caleb and Joshua that the land was "an exceeding good land" (Num. 14:7) were overridden by the rebels' misrepresentations.

First, they said the land "eateth up the inhabitants thereof" (13:32), but in the same sentence they spoke of all the people they saw. How could they have seen all these people if the land had eaten up all the people who lived there? Then, the ten twist-history rebels talked about the fact that they saw the giants and that every person they saw was a giant. This is unlikely, if even possible, because in all the reporting about the cities and inhabitants and people in the Book of Joshua, there are only isolated references to giants in the land one generation later.

After that twist, the spies said they were grasshoppers in the sight of all the people who saw them. Again, this is unlikely, since there is no record that anyone attempted to stalk them, hurt them, capture them, kill them or otherwise hinder their spying expedition. Had these twelve spies been as grasshoppers in the sight of the land's inhabitants, they would have been chased out at the least. It is much more likely that the inhabitants of the land had a fear of Israel because news of the plagues and the Exodus and the parting of the Red Sea had most surely reached them by this time, as Rahab was later to testify (Josh. 2:9–11).

This occasion of twist-history rebellion was swift in its development and also swift in its outcome. Joshua and Caleb sought to avert the disaster of unbelief, even to the point of commanding the people, "Only rebel not ye against the LORD, neither fear ye the people of the land; for they are bread for us:

their defence is departed from them, and the LORD is with us: fear them not" (Num. 14:9). Sadly, all because of the twist-history rebellion of ten men, the Exodus generation went to bed as "would nots" and woke up the next morning as "could nots."

The King of Ammon

Jephthah had an inglorious beginning, coming upon the scene as the son of Gilead by fornication; and, because of his tainted origins, his brethren hated him and cast him out, saying, "Thou shalt not inherit in our father's house; for thou art the son of a strange woman" (Judg. 11:2). This man rose above the unsavory criticisms levied at him. God called him "a mighty man of valour" in verse 1 and included him in His hall of faith in Hebrews 11:32. At the time that he was recalled to be the captain and judge of Israel, the Ammonites (ever enemies of God's people) were the chief oppressors.

Jephthah's first effort in dealing with the Ammonites was to bring peace without combat. He "sent messengers unto the king of the children of Ammon, saying, What hast thou to do with me, that thou art come against me to fight in my land?" (vs. 12). In the next verse, the Ammonite king outlandishly lied, showing what a twist-history rebel he was. He presented a completely false position when he said that Israel had stolen Ammonite land at the end of the wilderness wanderings just prior to the conquest of Canaan under Joshua.

While Jephthah was the son of a harlot and an emotionally unstable individual, he was also a good student of history. He knew the real chronology of events as recorded in the writings of Moses, the man of God, in Numbers 21:21–31. Jephthah knew that Moses had requested permission to pass through the land of Sihon, king of the Amorites, but that Sihon had responded in distrust and anger by attacking Israel at Jahaz. Jephthah knew that Moses had been decisively victorious and that God had rewarded Moses and the people of

Israel with the land "from Arnon unto Jabbok, even unto the children of Ammon: for the border of the children of Ammon was strong" (vs. 24). Jephthah knew that the people of Israel had exulted in their victory chants of "Woe to thee, Moab! thou art undone, O people of Chemosh: he hath given his sons that escaped, and his daughters, into captivity unto Sihon king of the Amorites" (vs. 29).

Because Jephthah knew his real history, he was able quickly and accurately to send answer back to the twist-history rebel king of Ammon. This he did, rehearsing Moses' request, the denial, the battle and the victory that Jehovah God had given. He then gave the king of Ammon a *precise observation,* a *poignant question,* and a *powerful conclusion:*

> "*So now the* LORD *God of Israel hath dispossessed the Amorites from before his people Israel, and shouldest thou possess it?*
>
> "*Wilt not thou possess that which Chemosh thy god giveth thee to possess? So whomsoever the* LORD *our God shall drive out from before us, them will we possess.*"—Judg. 11:23, 24.

When Jephthah had finished setting the record straight, he mentioned the three hundred years of interval between Moses' victory and Jephthah's present time, during which the children of Ammon had not recovered the disputed land. The upshot of Jephthah's entire dissertation was that he had not sinned against the king of Ammon, but that the king of Ammon was the one doing the wrong and that the Lord would be Judge of right and wrong. "So Jephthah passed over unto the children of Ammon to fight against them; and the LORD delivered them into his hands" (vs. 32). This twist-history king of Ammon and his idol-trusting, rabble-rousing underlings had attempted to remove the ancient landmark of truth about the land. Truly, Jephthah "subdued kingdoms, wrought righteousness...waxed valiant in fight, [and] turned to flight the armies of the aliens" (Heb. 11:33, 34).

The Jews Which Were of Asia

Whether revival or riot, Paul the apostle could be counted upon to create a stir wherever he went. His conversion in the city of Damascus was the first of many dramatic events that became the substance of his earthly sojourn for the Lord Jesus Christ. During his first visit to Jerusalem after his salvation (Acts 9:27, Gal. 1:18), the Lord came to Paul while he was in a trance and said, "Make haste, and get thee quickly out of Jerusalem: for they will not receive thy testimony concerning me" (Acts 22:18). Even with this warning directly from the Holy Spirit of God, the zealous apostle of the Gentiles still had an all-consuming passion for his Jewish brethren to the point of wishing that he himself could be "accursed from Christ for [his] brethren, [his] kinsmen according to the flesh" (Rom. 9:3). It was that obsession, that pressure in his spirit, that brought him back to Jerusalem after his third missionary journey.

Upon Paul's arrival in Jerusalem for that particular occasion, he gathered with the pastor, the apostle James, and the believers and "declared particularly what things God had wrought among the Gentiles by his ministry" (Acts 21:19). Paul's miracle-studded testimony evoked many praises among the Christians. Then, the leaders entered into dialogue with Paul to persuade him to conduct himself in accord with the Jewish law so as not to offend the Jews gathered at Jerusalem at the Feast of Pentecost (20:16). Paul agreed to shave his head and to enter into the temple with four other men who presumably had sworn a Nazarite vow and were bringing the required offering after having shorn their heads. In Paul's mind, he was fulfilling what he wrote to the Corinthians: "Unto the Jews I became as a Jew, that I might gain the Jews" (I Cor. 9:20). In the minds of the believers at Jerusalem, this public display was Paul's opportunity to convince the Jews that "those things, whereof they were informed concerning thee, are nothing; but that thou thyself also walkest orderly, and keepest the law" (Acts 21:24). In essence, Paul was helping the believing church at Jerusalem appease the tensions between Christian Jews and Orthodox Jews.

All went well until the seventh day of the feast, when the rebellious, twist-history "Jews which were of Asia...saw him in the temple" and cried out "Men of Israel, help: This is the man, that teacheth all men every where against the people, and the law, and this place: and further brought Greeks also into the temple, and hath polluted this holy place" (vss. 27, 28). Their agitated cry and the uproar that they instigated all developed because of a false understanding, a twisted history, if you will, of a past event. Verse 29 reveals that because they had seen Paul in Jerusalem with Trophimus, a Gentile Ephesian, they "supposed" Paul had also brought Trophimus into the temple, thus defiling it.

The underlying fact is that the Jews wanted a case against Paul. Twist-history rebels—like all rebels—do not need facts. They need twisted facts—facts that have been bent around to fit their rebel cause. There is neither scriptural nor secular record that Paul brought Trophimus the Ephesian into the temple, but such a twisted story suited the rebellious Jews who were desperate to find a flaw in Paul. Therefore, they twisted the events of the past week of the Feast of Pentecost and turned what was intended to be a celebration into a fiasco. In truth, they fulfilled Proverbs 16:27, because the fire they started became a conflagration of jealousy and rage that consumed the city.

Illustration

A couple had four sons and three daughters, in that order. The third son began to manifest discontent at about the age of seventeen, but nothing that anyone who knew him would classify as rebellion showed up until he was well into his twenties.

One summer at the family reunion, he suddenly brought up events from his childhood that left all his siblings and both parents aghast. As he insisted that this and that had happened, one by one the siblings spoke up and gave witness as to the impossibility of such incidents. Over and over, the one son maintained things that all six siblings and both parents knew were not true. He was twisting history. Later, it was discovered that he was seeking a way to justify some behavior that had caused him damage in the legal, civil, economic and social realms. He wanted to be able to turn history around and give the impression of having been mistreated and unloved so that he could convince himself—and others—that he was *simply* reacting to pain and suffering.

The Rule That the Righteous Live By

Sovereignty

God is sovereign over the affairs of men. In his sovereignty, God weaves together in His infinite wisdom both the events that He ordains as well as the events that He permits. Beyond that, God oversees the very individuals with whom a person will come into contact in his or her life. This amazing combination of people and happenings makes up a life. The righteous believer lives his life recognizing and accepting the sovereign rule and leading of God.

When a righteous believer is settled on the matter of God's sovereign oversight of his life, he is able to view events and people as separate ingredients which when taken individually may be unpleasant, but which when taken collectively are good and profitable. "All things work together for good to them that love God, to them who are the called according to his purpose" (Rom. 8:28). God does not say in this verse that all things are good in themselves, but that together all things work for good. This promise is true in the life of any person who meets both conditions of loving God and following His call. Twist-history rebels do not love God and do not follow His call; therefore, they never get to see the marvelous intertwining and weaving of God's tapestry in their lives. Righteous Christians, on the other hand, do love God and follow His call, and they are privy to the Lord's secret.

Another way that righteous believers show that they accept the sovereignty of God is to acknowledge that everything that happens falls "out…unto the furtherance of the gospel" (Phil. 1:12). Again, this is true to the person who has learned to accept history and not twist it. History-twisters usually embellish the good and exaggerate the bad to make themselves look better. Paul did neither. He learned in pain and in pleasantness, in fasting and in feasting. He took the opportunities that God handed to him. He saw that there were sinners around him whether he was in the marketplace or the prisonhouse, in the agora or the arena. Therefore, it did not matter to him where his Master deemed it wise to send him. He saw the sinners who needed to hear the Gospel, not the circumstances that threatened to rob him of his joy.

Righteous children of God also show their submission to God's sovereign way when they view each part and the whole of life as means for God's glory, not their own. Many of the chapters of life are difficult, but God can be glorified through them. Testings come, and their purpose is God's greater glory. Waiting periods arrive, and their intent, in God's mind, is greater glory. Sorrows befall the believer, and, again, God uses them for His greater glory.

Had the ten spies seen life's happenings as working together for good, as opportunity to represent the true God to the heathen, and as avenues for God's glory, they would have marched into Canaan and conquered it before the day was over. Any person who wants to prosper has to come eventually to this rule of the righteous that says God is sovereign, He is in control and He knows best. The righteous believer can say with Dr. Robert Ketchum, "God is too loving to be unkind and too wise to make a mistake."

11
The All-Believers-Are-Equal Rule

"I said unto the fools, Deal not foolishly: and to the wicked, Lift not up the horn:

"Lift not up your horn on high: speak not with a stiff neck.

"For promotion cometh neither from the east, nor from the west, nor from the south.

"But God is the judge: he putteth down one, and setteth up another."—Ps. 75:4–7.

As indicated earlier, there is close correlation between chapter 9 and this one. The nuance of contrast is that, while chapter 9 addresses the they-can-why-can't-I rebel's belief that he should be able to do anything that someone else is called, equipped and authorized to do, this chapter deals with the corrupt all-believers-are-equal attitude that says those who actually are called, equipped and authorized by God are really self-exalted, self-promoting individuals who lift themselves up at the expense of the value of the rest of the body of Christ. Furthermore, while chapter 9 treats the subject of uncalled, unauthorized individuals who seek to lift themselves up to the point of an authorized call, this chapter addresses the rebels who seek to bring down those who are, in fact, promoted by God. Since God is the One who puts down one and sets up another, the all-believers-are-equal rebel is really saying that all other believers are equal, but that he himself is in God's stead to put down and set up. This rebel, even if he doesn't realize it, unashamedly places himself on a par with God, making himself equal with God.

Korah

Korah and his company of "two hundred and fifty princes...famous in the congregation, men of renown" (Num. 16:2) were certainly formidable and convincing. Rebels the world over love to rest securely in the ideas that might makes right, that number equals honor, and that accepted opinion overrules inconvenient truth. When Korah and his band of famous and elite men within the congregation stood against Moses, they utilized both *important position* and *imposing presence* to convince Moses and Aaron that they were wrong to "lift...[themselves] above the congregation of the LORD" (vs. 3). Their complaint was that all believers are equal and that Moses and Aaron were lifting themselves up to a position that made others unequal with them. In standing before God, a believer is like all other believers; but in calling and office, God makes differences. God called Moses and Aaron to fulfill certain official duties which He never allowed or expected any other congregation member to accomplish.

All Believers Are Equal, So Back Down

Korah's opening statement to Moses (and Aaron) was, "Ye take too much upon you" (vs. 3). His complaint was wrong in insinuating that the leaders had taken the official calling upon themselves. Moses certainly did not call himself; in fact, he resisted rather adamantly when God did call him, and later he complained that God called him to something he could not do. All-believers-are-equal rebels are prone to this type of statement which is designed to create doubts in the minds of leaders as to their qualifications in an effort to cause them to waffle a bit and back down.

All Believers Are Equal, So Step Down

Korah was wrong further because he sought to sidetrack the issue with his claim that "all the congregation are holy, every one of them, and the LORD is among them" (vs. 3). The holiness of the people and God's presence among them were not the issues; calling and office were the issues. All-believers-are-equal rebels are adept at clouding the issues with logical-sounding—and I might add spiritual-sounding—reasoning. The idea that since all believers are equal in God's sight in their standing, therefore all believers are also alike in God's sight in their office is false. This all-believers-are-equal rebellion is misused to demonstrate that no believer has any right to authority or leadership over any other believer. Korah's focus and purpose was to get Moses to step down. This, of course, would pave the way for Korah to step up, for no rebel is content until he has control.

The very essence of such an effort is rebellion. For Believer A to expect or demand that Believer B step down from the calling wherewith he was called is to expect or demand that Believer B rebel against the God whose "gifts and calling...are without repentance" (Rom. 11:29). The all-believers-are-equal rebel does not want all believers to be equal; in reality, he wants all other believers to be equal so he can be the "unequal" one. The rebel wants to be in charge. In his quest, then, he must diminish all those whom God has exalted with His high, holy, hope-filled calling (Eph. 4:4; II Tim. 1:9), reducing them to the mediocrity of the bland norm.

God is not in the business of putting men above others so they will be arrogant. Moses certainly was neither condescending nor arrogant, his meekness having already been established (Num. 12:3). Rather, God is in the work of elevating men to places of greater and greater responsibility and duty according to their faithfulness, so that their greater reward for such faithfulness at the judgment brings greater glory to Him.

All Believers Are Equal, So Come Down

When Moses challenged Korah and his men to "take...censers...And put fire therein, and put incense in them before the LORD" (16:6, 7) so as to let the Lord settle the issue, Korah answered Moses with a defiant "We will not come up" (vss. 12, 14). While this may be a play on words, it is also a biblical truth. All-believers-are-equal rebels will not come up; they want leaders to come down so *they* can then go up! Korah was urging Moses to dismount from what he perceived to be a high horse, when in all actuality, "the man Moses was very meek, above all the men which were upon the face of the earth" (12:3). It was not Moses who needed to acquire lowliness, meekness or humility. Rather, the rebels needed the big dose of those inner qualities.

Diotrephes

The tiny epistle of III John is addressed to "the well-beloved Gaius" and deals primarily with a problem the church was having with a man named Diotrephes. In brief but pointed language, the apostle whom Jesus loved outlined Diotrephes' attitude and actions which lucidly portray all-believers-are-equal rebellion.

All-Believers-Are-Equal Rivalry

Diotrephes was a man whose yearning for importance was obsessive to the point that he sought after what belongs solely to Christ: preeminence. Incidentally, the word "preeminence" is found only twice in the New Testament, here and in Colossians 1:18, where it is Christ whose seven-fold magnificence renders Him worthy "that in all things he might have the preeminence." Diotrephes placed himself in competition, in a rivalry, if you please, to attain what the Lord Jesus Christ was given from His Father. For Diotrephes to covet that which belongs solely to the risen, resurrected Lord Jesus Christ is the ultimate rivalry of all-believers-are-equal rebellion!

The preeminence of Jesus Christ is untouchable and intangible. Nothing that Diotrephes could ever do could damage the fact that Jesus Christ conquered death and ascended on high. However, he could damage the leaders that Jesus Christ commissioned and left behind, and he did his best at that. If ever a man wanted to pull down the called and anointed leaders—in this case the apostles—it was Diotrephes. His entire scriptural biography of two verses is riddled with evidences of his all-believers-are-equal rebellion in its expressions of rivalry against Christ, against John the aged apostle, and, by association, a transferred rivalry against all the apostles as the earthly representatives of Jesus Christ and against all whom the apostles would approve.

All-Believers-Are-Equal Rejection

Beyond his adversial competition against Christ and the apostles, Diotrephes refused to receive the apostles. Like his rivalry, his rejection also included others whom the apostles approved and sent, When John said that "Diotrephes...receiveth us not" (emphasis mine), he could not have been referring to himself and the other apostles, because all the other apostles were with the Lord by that time. John meant by the plural pronoun that this all-believers-are-equal rebel was rejecting John himself as well as any representative or emissary whom the aged apostle might deploy to the church for doctinal instruction, spiritual edification, authoritative correction or general ministration of any kind. Diotrephes' all-believers-are-equal rebellion despised the last apostle. Rather than welcome John and reap all that was possible from this eyewitness of the resurrection, he chose to reject him; and with that rejection, Diotrephes rejected all that John could offer of beneficial ministry and bona fide ministers.

All-Believers-Are-Equal Rantings

In addition to rejecting the apostles and their inspired communications, Diotrephes sought to equalize all believers by prating against John and his messengers; that is, by uttering foolish, endless nonsense about them. His prating had a particular quality that does not characterize all prating, that of malice. His pratings were filled with hatred and wrath and vengeance and ire, no doubt a living evidence of his long-suppressed anger that the apostles had been chosen and he had been bypassed.

All-Believers-Are-Equal Removals

Diotrephes was not content to rival, reject and rant on and on against the apostles in angry words; his rebellion was so rabid that he engaged in an activity totally unbecoming to any believer—the popish removal of people from the fellowship of the saints. Nowhere does God give any single man the authority to remove others from the assembly. When the church had to perform such a drastic measure, it was to be done "in the name of our Lord Jesus Christ, when [the church was] gathered together...with the power of our Lord Jesus Christ" (I Cor. 5:4). Instead of adhering to the apostolic directive, this man Diotrephes took upon himself the right of culling the membership in a papal pseudosupremacy that would never rest until all leadership other than his own was put down. Diotrephes did this by direct and indirect association. He would not himself receive the brethren. Anybody who was linked to or loyal to the apostles was forbidden to attend the church. Beyond that, anyone who would sympathize with those who were linked to or loyal to the apostles would be removed from the membership he already held.

Diotrephes was a dyed-in-the-wool all-believers-are-equal rebel. He wanted to pull down the entire biblical authority structure for the church that was "built upon the foundation of the apostles and prophets, Jesus Christ himself being the chief corner stone" (Eph. 2:20), so that he could elevate himself to preeminence. No wonder the aged apostle who ended his first epistle with the words, "Little children, keep yourselves from idols" (I John 5:21), said here, "Beloved, follow not that which is evil, but that which is good" (III John 11).

Illustration

A long-serving pastor who had the respect of both the church family and the community where he ministered was approached by a lady at the end of a service. This woman presented herself as willing to serve in the church. The pastor mentioned a variety of areas where this woman could invest her talents and help others. Strangely, the woman who had just presented herself withdrew her presentation and went her way.

Within a few weeks, this woman had surrounded herself with a few dissatisfied others within the assembly, and they all came together to meet the pastor. Thankfully, the pastor had sufficient spiritual insight and experiential wisdom to have two deacons present at the meeting. The woman served as the spokesperson for the gripers, even though there were three men on her bandwagon. Her voice became loud, her tone abrupt and her countenance cross. Her entire demeanor was rebellious as she laid out several egregious complaints against the pastor's ministerial qualifications, leadership capabilities and preaching style. She further stated that her desires to serve in that church were not for what she called menial tasks like nursery duty and Sunday school teaching but for what she termed *real* leadership.

One of the deacons was a man whom the pastor had brought to Christ, discipled and trained. The pastor had been instrumental in rescuing his shipwrecked marriage, restructuring his home and retarding the effects of rebellion in his children. This deacon spoke at length, with tears, and closed his testimony with the question, "In what way is this dear pastor not qualified or capable to lead?"

The woman and her cohorts were silenced, and miraculously, they never troubled the church again. She took her all-believers-are-equal band of rebels and hightailed it to another church, where within three months, she had sponsored a split and several other problems.

The Rule That the Righteous Live By

Inequality

While the all-believers-are-equal rebel sets himself up to be equal with God, the righteous believer knows and accepts full well that, for any mere man, it is "robbery to be equal with God" (Phil. 2:6). Rather than focus upon equality, the righteous live by the rule of inequality—inequality with God, that is. Instead of attacking God's leaders and demanding that they back down, step down and come down, the righteous believer sees himself and all other believers as under God, not equal with Him.

The inequality rule that righteous believers live by is found in Philippians 2:1–8, where Paul deals with the mind of the spiritual Christian. At the basic level of the believer's life, all consolation is in Christ, all comfort is the love of God, and all fellowship is that of the Holy Spirit of God (vs. 1). Righteous believers are focused upon magnifying Christ (1:20) and respecting others (2:2–4). In this portion, God says three things about the righteous believer's mind that will produce biblical inequality.

First, the Lord speaks of a mind *governed by love*: "Fulfil ye my joy, that ye be likeminded, having the same love, being of one accord, of one mind" (vs. 2). The more God's love fills the mind of the righteous believer, the more he sees himself and all others on the level ground at the foot of the cross. He sees God high and lifted up with His train filling the temple and the seraphim crying, "Holy, holy, holy" all around Him (Isa. 6:1, 3). As soon as the righteous believer consents to the rule of his own inequality with God, he is ready to be like-minded and in one accord with others, making no attempt to bring them down and every attempt to lift Christ up.

After that, the apostle Paul continued by mentioning a mind *geared toward lowliness*. "Let nothing be done through strife or vainglory; but in lowliness of mind let each esteem other better than themselves" (Phil. 2:3). In Korah or Diotrephes, there is not one shred of esteeming others as better than self. However, the righteous child of God who lives by the rule of inequality does so by raising others higher, not by raising himself higher.

There is a careful balance to be observed in this aspect of the lowly mind. One is "not to think of himself more highly than he ought to think; but to think soberly, according as God hath dealt to every man the measure of faith" (Rom. 12:3). A man should not puff up himself and consider himself better than everyone else, but one should also think soberly; that is, he should not deflate himself and consider himself worse than everyone else.

It is not spiritually healthy or wise to develop a worthlessness complex. Thinking soberly causes a righteous believer to view himself as unworthy of God's myriad blessings and gifts. Sober thinking, however, does not dwell upon worthlessness. The worth of any person or thing is determined by the price paid for it. Christ invested His lifeblood in every soul, thus giving each person inestimable value.

A mind geared toward lowliness is a mind that does not

limit itself to looking upon "his own things, but every man also on the things of others" (Phil. 2:4).

Finally, the righteous live by the rule of inequality by allowing their minds to be *guided by the Lamb*. Philippians 2:5 begins with the word "let" in the imperative mode. In command form, God says, "Let this mind be in you, which was also in Christ Jesus." Christ, having had eternal and perfect equality with the Father, put on the aura and nature of inequality when He "made himself of no reputation, and took upon him the form of a servant, and was made in the likeness of men" (vs. 7). Regardless of how worthy anyone deems himself to be, he cannot spiritually think of himself as better than or more worthy than Christ. If Christ, in His equality with God, humbled himself to "even the death of the cross" (vs. 8), so every believer in his inequality with God should humble himself to that "death" as well. This crucified life of the righteous believer is always a life lived by the rule of inequality with God.

12
The Blame-the-Righteous Rule

"Ye say, The way of the Lord is not equal. Hear now, O house of Israel; Is not my way equal? are not your ways unequal?"

"Yet the children of thy people say, The way of the Lord is not equal: but as for them, their way is not equal."—Ezek. 18:25; 33:17.

"But as then he that was born after the flesh persecuted him that was born after the Spirit, even so it is now."—Gal. 4:29.

Self-justification is a natural response to having one's sin exposed. One of the variant forms of this justification is called blame-shifting, a clever imputation of the rebel's blame to the account of one who is innocent of that blame. The rebel or group of rebels seldom applies the blame to a fellow rebel or group of rebels; instead, rebels seek out a spiritual individual or group upon whom to place blame. So it goes in keeping with this rebel rule to say that the righteous are to blame. Indeed, those who are in sin up to their ears love to blame those who are in sin up to their ankles!

In Ezekiel's day, the common people even dared to blame God Himself for the unequal things going on in their society. Talk about blaming the righteous! The nation had *rebelled through idolatry* and *reaped through captivity*. By the time

Ezekiel was God's spokesman, their embittered hearts had come to lay the blame upon God. There is none more righteous than the Lord, and the idolatrous Judeans were faulting Him! Apparently, they had not learned that he who faults God faults himself.

Korah, Dathan, Abiram and the Children of Israel

The children of Israel were murmurers and complainers par excellence! Their journey to Sinai and their wilderness wanderings were filled with alarming examples of rebellion. One such situation, the organized rebellion of Korah and Dathan and Abiram (see chapter 11) resulted in having the entire nation blame Moses.

Moses and Aaron were far from morally perfect, but in this instance they were faultless. Korah, Dathan and Abiram had organized a rebellious force of "two hundred and fifty princes of the assembly, famous in the congregation, men of renown" (Num. 16:2). It seems that this number was joined by more and more until much of the congregation's voice was behind them, because one result of Korah's gainsaying and God's sudden intervention was that "all the congregation of the children of Israel murmured against Moses and against Aaron, saying, Ye have killed the people of the LORD" (vs. 41).

The blame-the-righteous rebellion of the congregation developed in stages. The ringleaders, joined by two hundred fifty princes, accused Moses and Aaron, the righteous ones in this situation, of three main issues: (1) Moses and Aaron had exalted themselves over the people to keep the people under; (2) Moses and Aaron had brought the people to the wilderness to kill them; and (3) Moses and Aaron had failed to bring the people to a land of milk and honey. Korah and his cohorts worded their accusations in a manner that would *incline the congregation to their side* and *include the congregation in their scheme.* Each of these three main faults lodged against Moses and Aaron was expressed in terms of its ill effect upon the common people.

As is the case with all rebellion, truth got quite well hidden by the imagined injustices of the righteous against the rebels! Having heard such accusations as these, Moses (and Aaron) could have engaged in some well-justified retaliation. Instead, they remained righteous, manifesting meekness and employing intercession.

Blame the Righteous for Positional Troubles

Moses and Aaron had not lifted themselves up to their positions, nor had they pushed the people down to theirs. There is no evidence that Moses and Aaron sought to lift themselves above the congregation of the Lord to create a separation between clergy and laity. To the contrary, Jehovah God sent them to the leadership task of His design and by His choosing. God and God alone was responsible for the positions of Moses of Aaron, and the same God was responsible for the positions of Korah and his company and the positions of every other person in the congregation.

In response to this acid-tongued faultfinding, Moses invited Korah and his cohorts to "take...censers...And put fire therein, and put incense in them before the LORD" (vss. 6, 7) in a meek effort to allow God to show Himself. In no way did Moses intend to carry out his own vengeance. Moses even went as far as to ask Korah if he considered his position in "the service of the tabernacle of the LORD...to stand before the congregation to minister" (vs. 9) to be "a small thing." Moses further asked Korah if the fact that his tribe of Levi had been selected to approach the Lord was a low or insignificant thing. Of course, Korah and his company were not interested in getting themselves into the trouble of Nadab and Abihu, who had intruded into the priestly office (see chapter 9), nor were they disposed to answer Moses' soul-searching questions, so they abruptly declined his offer. "We will not come up" was their insolent response (vss. 12, 14) because they did not want the truth about their efforts to organize a blame-the-righteous rebellion to come out in public.

Blame the Righteous for Congregational Troubles

Along with their refusal of Moses' remedy for the controversy over leadership, Korah and his fellow blame-the-righteous rebels added their second accusation about Moses and Aaron trying to kill the people. This was absurd, because if Moses and Aaron had brought the Israelites to the wilderness to kill them, they would have allowed Pharaoh's army to do the job before they ever crossed the Red Sea!

True, Israel had encountered life-threatening conditions on many occasions—there had been times of no water, times of no food and times of no escape. Problems that seemed to threaten the very existence of the nation abounded. However, they did not die, because over and over God provided through the very leadership that Korah and his evil men were now criticizing. Instead of seeing the continuous and miraculous provisions of water, food and safety, Korah and his company opted to bring up the old saw that Moses and Aaron were attempting to kill them, which had been around since they had left Egypt (Exod. 16:3).

Blame the Righteous for Consequential Troubles

Korah's third fault against Moses and Aaron was that they had not brought them into the Promised Land and given them their inheritance but had doomed them to wander in the wilderness. The false idea that Moses and Aaron were keeping them from the Promised Land was ludicrous. These accusations were dead wrong, out of context and unreasonable. It was the congregation who murmured more than once that it would have been better for them to die in Egypt—a comment rooted in the faithless idea that they would die and never see Canaan! It was not Moses and Aaron who refused to give them the land and assign them their inheritance; the very rebels themselves had refused to go into that land in Numbers, chapters 13 and 14. It was not Moses and Aaron who had doomed them to death and forty years of wandering; God had pronounced that consequence as His divine response to their refusal to conquer when He had promised them victory!

In response to these revived lies, Moses again resorted to a meek approach. When Dathan and Abiram said that they would not come to meet with Moses, Moses simply resorted to prayer—albeit a prayer of righteous indignation—that God would not respect their offering (Num. 16:15). He then demanded that Korah and his company be before the Lord the following day.

It's easy to imagine that all that night, Korah and his company spread the word throughout the entire congregation. The accusations abounded from tent to tent. The rebellion rippled from tribe to tribe. At the dawn of the following day, Korah and his two hundred fifty princes "took every man his censer, and put fire in them, and laid incense thereon, and stood in the door of the tabernacle of the congregation with Moses and Aaron. And Korah gathered all the congregation against them unto the door of the tabernacle of the congregation" (vss. 18, 19). This cowardly approach brought God's intervention. God's glory came down to appear to the congregation, and the Lord was heard as He commanded Moses and Aaron, "Separate yourselves from among this congregation, that I may consume them in a moment" (vs. 21). Again, Moses responded in meekness, pleading for the deliverance of the congregation who had been led so far astray by such ill-fated men as Korah, Dathan and Abiram.

God, responding to Moses' plea, did not destroy the evil congregation. All that was left to do was to plead with the people to get away from the camp of Korah and the others so that God could at least do away with the *perpetrators* if not the *partners!* The ensuing scene again demonstrated Moses' righteous, gentle, nonvengeful spirit as he spoke to the congregation, commanding the people to remove themselves from the proximity of the ringleaders' tents. He reminded the people that he did not carry out his leadership out of his own mind, and announced the new thing of the earth's opening her mouth to swallow alive the ones who had so brazenly provoked the Lord (vs. 30). Of course, the words were no sooner out of Moses' mouth than "the ground clave asunder that was under them: And the earth opened her mouth, and swallowed them up, and their houses, and all the men that appertained unto Korah...went down alive into the pit, and the earth closed upon them: and they perished from among the congregation" (vss. 31–33). Immediately after this, "there came out a fire from the LORD, and consumed the two hundred and fifty men that offered incense" (vs. 35) in a fashion quite similar to God's sudden consumption of Nadab and Abihu in Leviticus 10.

All this is laid down for the student of Scripture. Moses was completely within the bounds of his responsibility. He was kind, meek, gentle and completely submissive to God—and righteous. Moses had "not taken one ass from them, neither [had he] hurt one of them" (vs. 15) in any manner. He and Aaron responded to the accusations, the *arrogance* and the *approach* of these wicked rebels with grace and prayer. He gave the rebels opportunity to think through their actions, realize the severity of their insurrection and back down. He interceded on behalf of the followers, begging God not to be so angry with the entire congregation for the sin of a few. He gave the congregation ample warning to remove themselves from the vicinity of the guilty ones. Then Moses stood back, and God stepped in.

The miracles of opening the earth to swallow some of the rebels and consuming the others with fire were from God, yet the congregation persisted in their blame-the-righteous rebellion by impugning Moses and Aaron for the deaths of the wicked. "Ye have killed the people of the LORD," they cried (vs. 41). It took the deaths of fourteen thousand seven hundred more of the children of Israel to quell the murmurings. From start to finish, Numbers 16 is a prime example of the way rebellious people deny their own part in organized rebellion and defy God's intervention against them and lay blame and responsibility upon God's righteous leaders.

King Ahab

Among individuals who display the blame-the-righteous rebellion, Ahab reigns supreme. Seemingly, his every encounter with Elijah was just another occasion or opportunity for his poisonous tongue to express this form of rebellion. Elijah was *called to stand in God's presence, commissioned to stand for God's precepts and commanded to stand against Ahab's perversion.*

And was Ahab ever perverse! He was perverse in his *ways,* doing "evil in the sight of the LORD above all that were before him" (I Kings 16:30). He was perverse in his *wedding,* taking "to wife Jezebel the daughter of Ethbaal king of the Zidonians" (vs. 31). He was also perverse in his *worship,* rearing "up an altar for Baal in the house of Baal" (vs. 32). God's conclusion about this perverse man is that "there was none like unto Ahab, which did sell himself to work wickedness in the sight of the LORD, whom Jezebel his wife stirred up. And he did very abominably in following idols" (21:25, 26). All this and more could be cited to demonstrate Ahab's rebellion.

The righteousness of Elijah is settled in God's simple intro-duction of His prophet: "And Elijah the Tishbite, who was of the inhabitants of Gilead, said unto Ahab, As the LORD God of Israel liveth, before whom I stand, there shall not be dew nor rain these years, but according to my word" (17:1). God declared this man, who appeared suddenly and eventually dis-appeared miraculously, to be one who stood in His presence. Probably Ahab thought Elijah to be a blustering fool, one of those ridiculous followers of Jehovah who were always trying to scare people into forsaking idols with their pronouncements of doom and trouble. So insignificant is Ahab's response, if he even had one, that God did not record it.

Blame the Righteous for National Troubles

When Ahab and Elijah next met, it had not "rained...on the earth by the space of three years and six months" (Jas. 5:17). The passage of three and a half years of time had caused Ahab to have a different take on this prophet who had so boldly declared the drought. Obadiah informed Elijah that in the interim between his first and second meetings with Ahab, "There is no nation or kingdom, whither my lord hath not sent to seek thee: and...he took an oath of the kingdom and nation, that they found thee not" (I Kings 18:10). Ahab desperately wanted to find Elijah to get him to reverse the drought, but certainly he did not want to repent of his deeds. Listen to Ahab's blame-the-righteous words: "Art thou he that troubleth Israel?" (vs. 17). Elijah set him straight by saying that he, the king, was the true troubler of Israel, along with all his father's house, because of their idolatry with Baal and their abandon-ment of Jehovah.

Blame the Righteous for Religious Troubles

The second time that Ahab manifested his blame-the-right-eous rebellion, Elijah was not present. This time, Ahab was conversing with his vicious wife, reporting to her "all that Elijah had done, and withal how he had slain all the prophets with the sword" (19:1). This conversation was not an excited reporting of Elijah's amazing sermon on Mt. Carmel, of his simple but powerful prayer over the sacrifice, of the fire of God that fell or of Elijah's patriotism and heroism for Israel. This was a report to his coiled-serpent wife in which he sought blantantly to lay upon Elijah not just the national problems and environmental plight, but now the blame for the deaths of four hundred fifty prophets of Baal.

Between this instance and the next meeting of Elijah and Ahab, the prophet Elijah ran for his life from Jezebel's threats and had his recommissioning service on Mount Horeb, while King Ahab led Israel—with encouragement from an unnamed prophet, a man of God—in two victorious routs over the nation of Syria. Following those victories, King Ahab spared King Benhadad, and one of the sons of the prophets told Ahab he would pay with his own life because he had spared Benhadad, a man whom the Lord had slated for death.

This news led Ahab into one of the pouts for which he was so well known. Perhaps thinking that a country retreat would enable him to bring himself out of the slough of his sin-spawned sulk, he decided to add Naboth's vineyard to his possessions; but even this did not work, and his despair deepened. When Jezebel finally intervened, she had Naboth stoned and the deed to his property granted to Ahab to comfort him.

Blame the Righteous for Personal Troubles

Following this event, the word of the Lord came to Elijah again. God told him to go meet Ahab "in the vineyard of Naboth, whither he is gone down to possess it" (21:18). Ahab's first words to Elijah are blame-the-righteous words if such words were ever spoken: "Hast thou found me, O mine enemy?" (vs. 20). Again, rather than accept his responsibility for wicked, murderous rebellion, he laid the guilt upon Elijah in an attempt to *salve his conscience* and *save his cause*. This time Elijah stayed around for a spell and pronounced a lengthy curse, telling Ahab that right where the dogs licked up the blood of Naboth they would lick up his blood, that his house was to be expunged from the earth just as the house of Jeroboam the son of Nebat had been, and that dogs would one day eat Jezebel by the wall of Jezreel. Such biting, pointed words caused King Ahab some pause, and "he rent his clothes, and put sackcloth upon his flesh, and fasted, and lay in sackcloth, and went softly" (vs. 27).

Blame the Righteous for All Troubles

No further encounters between Elijah and Ahab are recorded, but Ahab did not recover from his habit of thinking that trouble is always to be attributed to the righteous. Three years passed, and Syria had failed to recover enough military strength to reorganize against Israel. Ahab, the cowardly king of Israel, and Jehoshaphat, the compromising king of Judah, decided to take advantage of this weakness in their common rival to recover Ramoth in Gilead. The two kings sat together in the battle-planning days, surrounded by the four hundred prophets whose singular message was for Ahab to go up in this battle and prosper against Syria and recover this strategically located city for Israel. Jehoshaphat, compromiser though he was, still had enough conscience of Jehovah God to ask, "Is there not here a prophet of the LORD besides, that we might enquire of him?" (22:7). Ahab said, "There is yet one man…but I hate him; for he doth not prophesy good concerning me, but evil" (vs. 8). Down to the day before his death at the hands of the aimless, nameless bowman, Ahab was a man who felt that his own personal troubles, as well as his national troubles, were all the fault of the righteous preachers of the righteous message of the righteous God Jehovah.

Illustration

A godly lay youth leader had served in his country church and community for fourteen years. Due to the small size of his town, he was well known; and due to his honorable conduct, he was well respected. Believers and nonbelievers, members of his church and members of other churches and members of no church all respected him. A new family from a distant state moved to the town and began attending the church. On the next scheduled youth outing, the sixteen-year-old daughter of this new family was touched in an inappropriate manner by an unsaved seventeen-year-old who had been invited by a regular member of the youth group. The new parents raised a ruckus, started rumors and entered litigation against the youth leader for negligence of duty and ineptness (because he was not ordained). The upshot was that this well-respected, long-established servant of Christ was publicly shamed in the press, the church lost members and influence, and the young man who was really to blame (and his parents) were never even questioned or involved in any restitution of any kind. The entire fault was laid upon the righteous servant of God, while the true culprits were exonerated!

The Rule That the Righteous Live By

Confession

The righteous are quick to seek God and take what blame is theirs and confess their sins and iniquities. They live by the rule of confession, taking their burden of sin to the cross where it can be forgiven and where restoration can begin.

First, the righteous live by the rule of confession because they understand that they have sin in their nature and that they have sin in their lives. Rather than blame others for their circumstances and consequences, they look to the Scriptures to discern their own sins and iniquities and then look to God for restoration through the efficacious blood of Jesus Christ. Righteous believers do not deceive themselves by saying they have no sin, nor do they make God a liar by saying they have not sinned (I John 1:8–10). They "let God be true, but every man a liar...That [God might] be justified in [His] sayings" (Rom. 3:4).

The righteous believer also lives by the rule of confession because he knows it is the avenue to forgiveness. Blame-the-righteous rebels attempt to find release from guilt by placing false guilt upon others, but the righteous know that the only release from guilt is confession that brings forgiveness. Knowing that "he that covereth his sins shall not prosper: but whoso confesseth and forsaketh them shall have mercy" (Prov. 28:13), they willingly *face up* and *fess up* in order to have God's favor again. Their "godly sorrow worketh repentance...not to be repented of" (II Cor. 7:10), and they find *cleansing* and *clearing* for themselves. When the righteous are "made sorry after a godly manner, that [they] might receive damage...in nothing" (vs. 9), they demonstrate this rule by which the righteous live.

Again, righteous believers live by the rule of confession because of the promise of God's nearness to those who are contrite about sin. The most famous verse about contrition is Psalm 51:17: "The sacrifices of God are a broken spirit: a broken and a contrite heart, O God, thou wilt not despise." The psalmist also wrote, "The LORD is nigh unto them that are of a broken heart; and saveth such as be of a contrite spirit" (34:18). Isaiah, thought to be of aristocratic birth, did not let that stand between him and God but wrote that God dwells "in the high and holy place, with him also that is of a contrite and humble spirit" and "to this man will I look, even to him that is poor and of a contrite spirit, and trembleth at my word" (Isa. 57:15; 66:2). Confession that arises out of genuine sorrow and brokenness and tears about personal sin brings the tenderness of

God very near to the heart. Those who sense God as distant and aloof often find that their confession life is shallow. God is near to those who confess, and that is the reason the righteous live their lives by that rule.

13
The God's-Way-My-Way Rule

"I have not sent these prophets, yet they ran: I have not spoken to them, yet they prophesied.

"But if they had stood in my counsel, and had caused my people to hear my words, then they should have turned them from their evil way, and from the evil of their doings."

"For I have not sent them, saith the LORD, yet they prophesy a lie in my name; that I might drive you out, and that ye might perish, ye, and the prophets that prophesy unto you.

"Also I spake to the priests and to all this people, saying, Thus saith the LORD; Hearken not to the words of your prophets that prophesy unto you, saying, Behold, the vessels of the LORD'S house shall now shortly be brought again from Babylon: for they prophesy a lie unto you.

"Hearken not unto them; serve the king of Babylon, and live: wherefore should this city be laid waste?"

"For thus saith the LORD of hosts, the God of Israel; Let not your prophets and your diviners, that be in the midst of you, deceive you, neither hearken to your dreams which ye cause to be dreamed.

"For they prophesy falsely unto you in my name: I have not sent them, saith the LORD."—Jer. 23:21, 22; 27:15–17; 29:8, 9.

The God's-way-my-way rebel is a deceiver who pretends he wants to know and do God's will, but he actually wants to know God's will so he can perform it his own way. He knows the message of God. He knows some of the things God wants done. He knows God's Word enough to speak it and even quote it. But this rebel is unsent. God does not send him on the missions where he goes. This rebel goes on his own wherever he pleases and does his own thing under the guise of having the message and leading of God. Incidentally, God's message at the wrong time or in the wrong place is not God's message at all, but a message of rebellion against God's timing and placement.

Balaam, the Son of Beor

Balaam, the soothsayer (Josh. 13:22), was a God's-way-my-way rebel who is mentioned three times in the New Testament: II Peter 2:15, which mentions the "way of Balaam"; Jude 11, which speaks of the "error of Balaam"; and Revelation 2:14, which addresses the "doctrine of Balaam." Numbers 31:16 mentions the "counsel of Balaam." These specifics regarding this Old Testament rebel give understanding of what a God's-way-my-way rebel is like.

The student of Scripture finds fifty-one of the sixty-three references to Balaam in Numbers 22–24. At the time Balaam was alive and practicing his sorcery and witchcraft, Balak, the son of Zippor, was king of the Moabites. Having seen the vast multitude of Hebrews traversing the wilderness and having heard what Israel did to Sihon, king of the Amorites, and Og, king of Bashan, the Moabites were deathly afraid. For this reason, Balak sent servants from Moab and Midian to Balaam "with the rewards of divination in their hand" (22:7) to call Balaam to Moab to curse the Israelites. Balaam had a reputation that whomever he blessed was blessed and whomever he cursed was cursed. Balak had substantial reason to believe that his investment of gifts and money would not be wasted.

When Balak's servants arrived, Balaam showed hospitality and housed them for the night. In the night, God asked Balaam who the men in his house were, and he told the Lord they were servants of Balak who had come to ask him to come with them to curse a large multitude that had come out of Egypt. God told Balaam, "Thou shalt not go with them; thou shalt not curse the people: for they are blessed" (vs. 12). Regardless of anyone's attempt to "interpret" what God told Balaam, there is no exegetical sleight of hand that can change the facts. God wanted Balaam to have nothing to do with the servants of Balak, God did not want Balaam to go with them, and God most certainly did not want Balaam to curse Israel.

Balaam awoke in the morning and told Balak's servants, "The LORD refuseth to give me leave to go with you" (vs. 13). Those servants returned to their king empty-handed, so the king sent more honorable servants to solicit the cursing powers of the hireling prophet Balaam. This time Balaam's answer was, "I cannot go beyond the word of the LORD my God, to do less or more. Now therefore, I pray you, tarry ye also here this night, that I may know what the LORD will say unto me more" (vss. 18, 19). In this reply, Balaam was verbalizing the God's-way-my-way rebellion that was swelling within his heart. God had already told him not to go with the servants and not to curse the people. Balaam was fully aware of the commands, but he was seeking his own way to do what God had told him not to do.

God's-Way-My-Way Ways

The apostle Peter's second epistle addresses to a great degree the false teaching of the false apostles and false teachers whose Old Testament counterparts were the false prophets with their false prophecies. Second Peter 2:15, 16 says that such false apostles and teachers "have forsaken the right way, and are gone astray, following the way of Balaam the son of Bosor, who loved the wages of unrighteousness; But was rebuked for his iniquity: the dumb ass speaking with man's voice forbad the madness of the prophet." It is clear that

Balaam forsook God's right way for his own straying wrong way, that Balaam loved money regardless of its source, that Balaam's pursuit of God's-way-my-way rebellion was iniquity, and that Balaam's donkey was given a man's voice to reinforce God's forbidding of the false prophet's madness!

One may argue that God appeared to give Balaam permission to go with the men in Numbers 22:20 when he said, "If the men come to call thee, rise up, and go with them; but yet the word which I shall say unto thee, that shalt thou do." This was an example of God's allowing a man to do what that man was set to do. A similarity exists between this permission and God's seeming permission in Judges 20 for the obliteration of the tribe of Benjamin. God's will for Israel included all the tribes, but he allowed eleven tribes virtually to wipe out one because they were determined to do so. God responds this way to prove that He does not dictate to His people and to demonstrate that when people get what their carnality wants, they do not want what they get.

Balaam went, but "God's anger was kindled because he went" (Num. 22:22), and the angel of the Lord stood in the roadway with drawn sword. Obviously, Balaam's own way was not God's way. Seeing the angel, Balaam's donkey turned into a field, and Balaam smote his animal to return her to the roadway.

This time, the angel stood between two parallel vineyard walls where there was only a narrow passageway between the two adjoining properties. In order to pass the angel, the donkey had to squeeze against one of the walls; and in this effort, the donkey crushed Balaam's foot. Again, Balaam angrily struck his beast.

Finally, the angel stood where there was no possibility of passage, and the donkey simply fell down under Balaam. Balaam in anger again beat his animal, and God opened the donkey's mouth to ask Balaam why he had beaten her three times. Balaam responded that the donkey was mocking him and that he would kill her if he had a sword, so the donkey asked him if she had ever performed this way before, and Balaam said, "Nay." At this point, the Lord opened Balaam's eyes.

When Balaam and the angel with drawn sword made eye contact, Balaam bowed prostrate before him, something he had not done toward the Lord—God's-way-my-way rebels never bow to the Lord. The angel asked him why he had smitten his donkey and then said, "Behold, I went out to withstand thee, because thy way is perverse before me: And the ass saw me...unless she had turned from me, surely now also I had slain thee, and saved her alive" (vss. 32, 33). He then reiterated God's statement to Balaam as a last warning: "Go with the men: but only the word that I shall speak unto thee, that thou shalt speak" (vs. 35).

When God knows a man is determined to do something wrong, He seeks to stop that man with direct commands and clear instructions. When that man is still decisive in his heart to pursue what is wrong, God goes ahead of him to provide adverse circumstances that should stop him. When God perceives that the man will not be stopped by command or difficulties, He lets that man have his way and brings the consequences of disobedience upon that man. God was merely telling Balaam, "Okay, if you are bound and determined to go, then go; but you'd better not say anything except what I tell you to say."

All this makes it clear that God's-way-my-way rebellion is not God's way after all, but that it is a perverse way, a way of iniquity, a way that earns rebuke.

God's-Way-My-Way Reward

Jude, the brother of James and half-brother of the Lord Jesus Christ, also references how similar the New Testament false apostles and teachers are to Balaam. In Jude 11, he pronounced a woe upon the false apostles and teachers who "ran greedily after the error of Balaam for reward." From the texts already cited, it is clear that the reward of Balaam was the reward of divination, enchantments, curses and soothsaying and that the reward of Balaam was definitely not the reward of building gold, silver and precious stones upon the foundation of God (I Cor. 3:12)!

Balaam's answer to the angel (not to God) is typical of God's-way-my-way rebels: "I have sinned; for I knew not that thou stoodest in the way against me: now therefore, if it displease thee, I will get me back again" (Num. 22:34). There was no *if* about it! That is just the point of God's-way-my-way rebellion. It is a whittling away at God, a chiseling away at His direct command, a slow eroding of His absolutes. It was at this point that the angel repeated to Balaam that he should go with the men but speak only what he told him to speak. Balaam went and met Balak and then went with Balak "up into the high places of Baal" (vs. 41).

Numbers 23 records Balak's building of seven altars for the offering of seven oxen and seven rams in the "high places of Baal." While Balak stood by the offered animals, Balaam went to a high place, and God met with him and put into his mouth a parable of blessing to utter in favor of Israel. Balaam returned to Balak and gave the blessing, saying "How shall I curse, whom God hath not cursed? or how shall I defy, whom the LORD hath not defied" (vs. 8). Balaam went on to speak of the numerical multiplication of this grand nation until Balak interrupted him and rebuked him for blessing those whom he had hired him to curse. Balaam, of course, said that he had to speak what God put into his mouth.

God's-Way-My-Way Error

It is necessary once again to cite Jude 11, where the Bible

student can find that false apostles and teachers hotly pursue "the error of Balaam." This error comes out in the second attempt of Balak to get Balaam to curse God's people. Balaam's error was that all sin must be cursed and that no sin can be forgiven. God's truth is that forgiven sin cannot be held against a person to condemn or curse him! Balak was frustrated after the first encounter of Balaam with Israel, but he brought Balaam to another place where he could see but a small portion of Israel encamped.

Again Balak prepared seven altars and stood by the offered oxen and rams while Balaam went off by himself to seek God's way. Again, God gave Balaam a parable of blessing to utter, and again he uttered it, saying, "God is not a man, that he should lie; neither the son of man, that he should repent: hath he said, and shall he not do it? or hath he spoken, and shall he not make it good?" (vs. 19). Balaam went on to say that God had seen neither iniquity nor perverseness in Israel and that the Lord was with Israel and that no enchantment or divination against them could prevail.

God's statement that he had "not beheld iniquity in Jacob, neither [had] he seen perverseness in Israel" (vs. 21) seems utterly contrary to His many rebukes of that nation. However, that statement of God is made as God saw Israel under the blood, redeemed, forgiven and covenanted to Him in marriage. Balaam, along with all false religionists with no comprehension of true salvation, could not see this glorious truth. For this reason, he continued to seek enchantments to curse Israel, but "the LORD thy God would not hearken unto Balaam; but the LORD thy God turned the curse into a blessing" (Deut. 23:5); and God "would not hearken unto Balaam; therefore he blessed you still" (Josh. 24:10).

Balak was now more than frustrated. In essence, he said, "If you're not going to curse them, at least don't bless them!" And,

of course, Balaam said again that he had to say what God told
him to say. In anger, Balak built seven more altars and offered
seven more oxen and seven more rams. This time, Balaam did
not go off by himself "as at other times, to seek for enchantments" (Num. 24:1); he simply looked toward the wilderness
and uttered another parable of blessing by the Spirit of God.
Balak's anger was greatly enflamed by this time, and he told
Balaam to get back home without the honors that he would
have given him. At this juncture, Balaam manifested his God's-
way-my-way rebellion in its most defiant form when he
answered again that he could speak nothing but what the Lord
told him to say, and then went beyond what God told him to
say because of his lust for reward.

God's-Way-My-Way Doctrine and Counsel

Three times Balak attempted to get Balaam to curse Israel,
but God would not allow that. God even stooped to come to
Balaam at the site of Baal's altar to tell him what to say. God
even spoke to a perverted soothsayer to make sure he did not
utter a curse upon Israel. However, Balaam's way from the
moment he left his house was not God's way—it was Balaam's
way. When his foot was crushed between his donkey's rib ca ge
and the vineyard wall, he pressed on. When his donkey spoke
to him, he was unalarmed (because the Devil often empowers
animals to address people through soothsaying). When the
enchantments he sought all turned about into blessings, he
was unchanged. He was a rebel who insisted upon following
God's way his way.

However, when Balak angrily told Balaam to take a hike,
Balaam's love of reward took over, and he pulled Balak aside
and told him how he could defeat the Israelites. He did this in
direct disregard to the restriction placed upon him by the
angel who told him at the beginning of his rebellious journey:
"Go with the men: but only the word that I shall speak unto

thee, that thou shalt speak" (22:35). Numbers does not record the whole of his conversation with Balak, but additional texts tell us what Balaam told the king. Numbers 25:1, 2 say that "Israel abode in Shittim, and the people began to commit whoredom with the daughters of Moab. And they called the people unto the sacrifices of their gods." Then, Numbers 31:16 says, "Behold, these caused the children of Israel, through the counsel of Balaam, to commit trespass against the LORD in the matter of Peor." Psalm 106:28, in divine commentary on this event, says, "They joined themselves also unto Baal-peor, and ate the sacrifices of the dead." Revelation 2:14 gives further Spirit-inspired insight in its description of some in the church of Pergamos who held "the doctrine of Balaam, who taught Balac to cast a stumblingblock before the children of Israel, to eat things sacrificed unto idols, and to commit fornication."

In self-willed, God's-way-my-way rebellion, Balaam uttered words to Balak that God did not authorize him to speak. God did not speak to Balaam so that he could teach Balak the way to corrupt Israel. This was Balaam's God's-way-my-way expression of an inner rebellion that had not been quelled by a sword-wielding angel, by a talking donkey or by obvious revelation of what God's will toward Israel actually was. For that reason, Balaam taught Balak that, even though he himself could not destroy Israel, he could introduce idolatry and fornication to them so that their God would destroy them. In the plague caused by the idolatrous feast and its subsequent sordid orgy, twenty-four thousand souls died at the hand of God.

Astounding as it may seem that God would speak through Balaam, it is true that He did speak through him on certain occasions. However, as a *soothsayer* and a *gainsayer*, Balaam was not accustomed to God's speaking through him. He was familiar with the occult and the voices of the dead and of the spirits of unclean devils. The fact that he received two of the four messages from God "falling into a trance, but having his eyes open" (Num. 24:4, 16) is evidence that he was not prone to proper approach to God. Any Bible reader can compare the visions of God received by such holy seers as Moses, Isaiah, Ezekiel and Daniel and observe that these men were on their faces in humility before the great God of all, not standing about with their eyes open! The reason for the godly prophets' face-down, eyes-closed approach to God is that no man can see God and live.

Balaam's method of receiving visions was brazen and proud, just like the demons who assisted him in giving him the information he divined. Quite likely, Balaam's visions were generally more in the realm of that received by Eliphaz the Temanite in Job 4:12–20 where the passing by of a spirit caused his hair to stand up and where he could not discern the form of the image.

The visions that the true God gave to men are unlike this unholy vision given to a man who did not speak aright concerning God. In the visions God gave, there were intricate details about the appearance of God, and the prophets were focused upon bowing low and showing reverence, not on having their eyes open and watching their hair stand up!

The *ultimate message* of all God's-way-my-way rebellion is that those who cannot be cursed can be corrupted. The *ultimate result* of all God's-way-my-way rebellion is that those who cannot be cursed are corrupted, vexed with the wiles and beguilements of false gods and fornication (Num. 25:18). The *ultimate tragedy* of all God's-way-my-way rebellion is that corrupted souls end up either chastened unto death or defiled in heart and soul for life.

Illustration

An eight-year-old boy came forward one night at a missions conference to answer God's prompting and present himself to God for service. In his own words on the decision card, he said, "I came forward tonight to say to God that He can do what He wants to do with me, as long as it is on the mission field." While some with more maturity felt he should not "enclose" God by the requirement of the mission field, all at the meeting understood the sincerity and innocence of this young man's surrender.

By the time he was in his junior year of college, he was well on his way to the fruition of that commitment made over a decade prior. Then he met a young lady who wanted God to use her but did not sense God's call to a mission field. The young man's pastor, parents, college professors and friends all counseled him that her different direction was the closing of the door on their courtship. He felt he could do God's will his own way. After the wedding, he began to press her to go with him to the mission field. She resisted, saying he knew her heart before he married her. Today, they are casualties, statistics on the list of those who used to serve God.

The Rule That the Righteous Live By

Submission

Hymn writer C. Austin Miles, in his renowned hymn "Submission," penned these poignant words: "Though not the way I'd choose, in my way I might lose the joy that yet for me awaits." How true it is that the righteous believer is a surrendered, submitted soul who lets God have His way, His way. The previous sentence may look like a typographical error, but the repetition of the final two words is intentional. It is not enough to want God's way my way; the righteous believer must want God's way His way. The rule of submission, taking orders and commands from the mouth of God rather than from the mouth of man, will ensure that God's way is done God's way.

This rule of the righteous is illustrated in the life of Paul the apostle. At a crucial juncture in the ministry of Paul, Silas and Timothy, and after the decrees from the church at Jerusalem had been delivered to the Gentile churches, Paul needed clarity as to what God wanted for him. A God's-way-my-way rebel might have said that Paul could preach anywhere and see fruit. But Paul lived by the rule of submission. For that reason, he was "forbidden of the Holy Ghost to preach the word in Asia," and when "they assayed to go into Bithynia...the Spirit suffered them not" (Acts 16:6, 7). These closed doors were evidence of Paul's submission, because God's-way-my-way rebels like Balaam have no regard for closed doors, pushing them open at will, and all in the name of doing what God wants!

One night after the doors had closed, as Paul and Silas and Timothy had traveled as far as Troas, "a vision appeared to Paul." In this vision, "there stood a man of Macedonia, and prayed him, saying, Come over into Macedonia, and help us" (vs. 9). Paul's submissive spirit had been amply rewarded, "and after he had seen the vision, immediately we endeavoured to go into Macedonia, assuredly gathering that the Lord had called us for to preach the gospel unto them" (vs. 10). The words "assuredly gathering" tells us that Paul concluded with assurance what God's will was. Paul knew he had God's way, God's way, because He had confirmed it. The righteous live by the rule of submission to God's way in all their matters.

On another occasion, Paul wrote of his prayers that he "might have a prosperous journey by the will of God" (Rom. 1:10) to visit Rome. It is not until one compares other Scriptures that one can comprehend the weight of that decision upon the mind of Paul as he diligently waited for God's exact timing for such a journey. In Acts 19:21, he said, "I must also see Rome." In the closing of his Epistle to the Romans, Paul gets candidly personal about the whole matter:

> *"For which cause also I have been much hindered from coming to you.*
>
> *"But now having no more place in these parts, and having a great desire these many years to come unto you;*
>
> *"Whensoever I take my journey into Spain, I will come to you: for I trust to see you in my journey, and to be brought on my way thitherward by you, if first I be somewhat filled with your company.*
>
> *"But now I go unto Jerusalem to minister unto the saints."*
>
> *"When therefore I have performed this, and have sealed to them this fruit, I will come by you into Spain.*
>
> *"And I am sure that, when I come unto you, I shall come in the fulness of the blessing of the gospel of Christ."—* 15:22–25, 28, 29.

That Paul yearned strongly to get to Rome where he could minister to those believers is very obvious. That he had this inner compulsion for years is equally evident. What is sublime in Paul's scattered mention of this Spirit-led constraint is his utter willingness to wait for God's clear direction, exact timing and definite blessing. Paul did not want God's way his way. He wanted God's way, God's way. For that reason, his ministry in Rome was singularly blessed. God's way, God's way is the rule by which the righteous live.

One can only conjecture, but we wonder whether if Balaam had never gone to Balak, a true prophet might have caused God's people to hear His words and turned them from evil toward righteousness. It appears that a God's-way-God's-way servant of Jehovah might have averted the intermarriages, the idolatry, the fornication, the plague and the generational scars of Balaam's rebellion.

14
The I-Want-What-I-Want Rule

"And he said unto him, Went not mine heart with thee, when the man turned again from his chariot to meet thee? Is it a time to receive money, and to receive garments, and olive-yards, and vineyards, and sheep, and oxen, and menservants, and maidservants?"—II Kings 5:26.

"(For after all these things do the Gentiles seek:) for your heavenly Father knoweth that ye have need of all these things.
"But seek ye first the kingdom of God, and his righteousness; and all these things shall be added unto you."—Matt. 6:32, 33.

"Let your conversation be without covetousness; and be content with such things as ye have: for he hath said, I will never leave thee, nor forsake thee."—Heb. 13:5.

God is not against His people having things, but He is most adamantly against things having His people. I-want-what-I-want rebellion is a covetous manifestation that is not content with the *timing*, the *terms* or the *type* of God's provision. This brand of rebellion sees what it wants, wants what it wants, and gets what it wants, regardless of whether or not God may be pleased. When Colossians 3:5 refers to "covetousness, which is idolatry," the Holy Spirit settles once and for all that an I-want-what-I-want rebel is an idolator in the sense that he puts the *accumulation of what he wants* ahead of the *acceptance of what God wants*.

Achan

The preparation of Joshua for the conquest of Canaan was extensive. He was Moses' chief general in the war with Amalek in Exodus 17. In this book, he was also noted as Moses' "minister" and "servant" (24:13; 33:11). In Numbers, Joshua was one of the two faithful spies who gave a good report of the Promised Land. After Moses gave his last counsels to Israel, he charged Joshua with the leadership of God's people in their occupation of Canaan and in the division of the land by lots to the tribes. In that charge, he commanded Joshua,

> *"Be strong and of a good courage: for thou must go with this people unto the land which the LORD hath sworn unto their fathers to give them; and thou shalt cause them to inherit it.*
>
> *"And the LORD, he it is that doth go before thee; he will be with thee, he will not fail thee, neither forsake thee: fear not, neither be dismayed."*—Deut. 31:7, 8.

Once Moses, the man of God, died, God gave Joshua a similar charge.

> *"Be strong and of a good courage: for unto this people shalt thou divide for an inheritance the land, which I sware unto their fathers to give them.*
>
> *"Only be thou strong and very courageous."*
>
> *"Have not I commanded thee? Be strong and of a good courage; be not afraid, neither be thou dismayed: for the LORD thy God is with thee whithersoever thou goest."*—Josh. 1:6, 7, 9

After the miraculous passage over the Jordan River and the sanctified establishment of the memorial heaps of stones, Joshua then oversaw the circumcision of the new generation. Encamped at Gilgal, they kept the Passover in the new land, and the manna ceased to be provided. As Joshua viewed the coming conquests, he went abroad out of the camp to be alone near Jericho, and there the "captain of the host of the LORD" (5:14) met with Joshua. As Moses had done at the hallowed site of the burning bush, so did Joshua, loosing his shoes and bowing face forward to the earth in the presence of Almighty God.

God gave Joshua specific instructions regarding the attack on Jericho, the first city to be taken in the Promised Land. The men of war were to surround the city. Each day for six days, seven priests blowing trumpets of rams' horns and presumably the normal four priests bearing the ark of the covenant were to follow a silent, solemn procession of the men of war around the city one time, with a rear guard following the ark. On the seventh day, they were all to walk around the city in this manner seven times. At a given moment, the priests were to sound with the horns, the people were to shout with a great shout, and the wall of the city was to fall flat.

On that seventh morning, all protocol and procedure having been followed day by day for six days, the people did as Joshua commanded. After the seventh time around the city,

> *"When the priests blew with the trumpets, Joshua said unto the people, Shout; for the LORD hath given you the city.*
>
> *"And the city shall be accursed, even it, and all that are therein, to the LORD....*
>
> *"And ye, in any wise keep yourselves from the accursed thing, lest ye make yourselves accursed, when ye take of the accursed thing, and make the camp of Israel a curse, and trouble it.*
>
> *"But all the silver, and gold, and vessels of brass and iron, are consecrated unto the LORD: they shall come into the treasury of the LORD."*—6:16–19.

At that moment, as God had said, the walls fell down flat, and the Israelites took the city. The two spies who went into the land rescued Rahab and her household of faith. Then all the remaining men and women of any age along with all the animals were destroyed with the edge of the sword. Next, the gold, silver, brass and iron were brought forth for God's treasury, and the city was burned to the ground. After all this, Joshua cursed the city, saying that any person who would ever rebuild that city would lose his firstborn son in the laying of its foundation and his youngest son in the setting of its gates (vs. 26).

Unmentioned in the record of Joshua 6 is that in the process of bringing the precious metals out of the city, a man named Achan "saw among the spoils a goodly Babylonish garment, and two hundred shekels of silver, and a wedge of gold of fifty shekels weight [and] coveted them, and took them; and…hid [them] in the earth" (7:21) under his tent.

When the Lord told Joshua that Jericho was "accursed…to the LORD" and "consecrated unto the LORD" (6:17, 19), He meant that anything in it would be a curse to any man, even though the precious things were holy to God. In the conquest of Canaan, Jericho was a picture of the tithe and firstfruits which belong exclusively to God. When the tithe is rendered to the Lord, that tenth becomes a blessing. When it is kept, it becomes a curse to the man keeping it. When the firstfruits were waved and heaved up unto the Lord, they became a blessing; if they were kept, they were a curse. Furthermore, the curse upon the rebuilding of Jericho pictures the curse upon any man who would give his tithe or render his firstfruits and then take them back. Achan's covetous I-want-what-I-want rebellion, indeed his curse, is announced in Joshua 7:1: "But the children of Israel committed a trespass in the accursed thing: for Achan…took of the accursed thing."

Following that statement, Joshua 7 records Israel's fateful failure at the hands of a frail force at Ai, Joshua's desperate plea before God for Israel, God's rebuke of Joshua's prostration at a time when separation and cleansing were the needs, and God's exposure of Achan's (Israel's) sin. God specifically outlined what Achan did, saying he had "taken of the accursed thing...stolen, and dissembled also, and...put it even among [his] own stuff" (vs. 11).

I-Want-What-I-Want Taking

God said that Achan took the accursed thing, adding that he had stolen it. When Achan was selected out of his family the next morning, he admitted to the crime, saying that he took the things which he saw. I-want-what-I-want rebels are thieves, taking what they see, taking what belongs to others, taking even what belongs to God.

I-Want-What-I-Want Treachery

The next word that God used about Achan's I-want-what-I-want rebellion was "dissembled," a word that combines the meanings of hypocrisy and falsehood with the meanings of concealment and disguise. When this type of rebel is active in a situation, he often does not reveal his true motives by his actions. His craft and treachery are so well-planned and his mode of operation so well-oiled that no one on the outside can discern what is happening. Quite obviously, Joshua did not pray about his advance against Ai, but had he done so, it is likely God would have revealed the sin in the camp before the shameful defeat at Ai and deaths of thirty-six unsuspecting Israelite soldiers. Still, Joshua was a man of God, a leader with godly discernment and spiritual aptitude. For Achan to have slipped this treachery past his leader demonstrates that Achan was adept at dissembling.

I-Want-What-I-Want Title

Finally, Achan's rebellion showed up in the fact that he put what he had treacherously taken among his own stuff. He did not share it or spread it around. It was buried under *his* tent—all of

it, every item of it! From taking to treachery to entitlement—
such is the subtle process in the thinking of an I-want-what-I-
want rebel. Either in the act of treacherous taking or soon after-
ward, Achan convinced himself that he deserved what he had
acquired by dissembling and dishonesty. Because he rationalized
in his rebellious heart that he had title to such possession, he
committed the act. Because he knew in his rebellious heart that
he had no title to such possession, he covered the act. His
untimely death and the unnecessary deaths of others resulted
from his living out the covetous I-want-what-I-want rule of
rebellion.

Gehazi

In the miracle-laden days of Elijah and Elisha, the latter
employed an assistant by the name of Gehazi, mentioned primarily in II Kings 4 and 5. In the early days of Gehazi's servitude to Elisha, he was blameless, helping the prophet at every
opportunity. So blameless was he that he was asked to be
involved even in the specific aspects of Elisha's ministry to the
great woman of Shunem. On the day that Elisha pronounced
that this great woman would have a son, Gehazi was there.

I-Want-What-I-Want Carelessness

Some years later, that son suddenly became ill and died.
Distraught, the grief-stricken mother took the boy's limp body
up to the bedchamber of Elisha and then set out in haste to
find the prophet. The time that had elapsed in the growing of
the child was the same time span in which Gehazi became
careless about his spiritual life and calling to help Elisha. When
this sorrowing woman of Shunem approached Elisha for help
about her dead son, Gehazi attempted to push her away. From
being blameless, he had digressed from God in his personal
life to a place of carelessness. His inability to discern the distress and the brokenness of this woman, and his calloused

reponse to her were due to the rising up in his heart of I-want-what-I-want rebellion. I-want-what-I-want rebellion often manifests itself in an uncaring attitude toward anyone who is not a "gold mine," and it is perhaps for that reason that he thrust her away from Elisha. He saw this great woman as one who had nothing to give except for a bed, a table, a stool and a candlestick (II Kings 4:10). It took Elisha's sensitivity to the Lord to override Gehazi's careless apathy.

I-Want-What-I-Want Powerlessness

Those who are guilty of *covetous possessiveness* are soon the victims of *embarrassing powerlessness*. When Elisha sent Gehazi to the great woman's home to lay his staff upon the child, nothing happened. It took Elisha's personal visit and a rather protracted series of Elisha's stretches and pacings to and fro along with the child's sneezes before the child finally opened his eyes and Elisha presented him to his mother alive and well. Gehazi seems to have been so eaten with covetous greed by this time that he had no power to perform for God, to say nothing of his inability to serve his master upon earth.

I-Want-What-I-Want Faithlessness

Some time later in Elisha's ministry, he had occasion to take a small portion of bread and corn to feed a hundred men. Gehazi, called Elisha's "servitor" in that passage, asked, "What, should I set this before an hundred men?" (vs. 43). He had moved from being powerless to being faithless. His I-want-what-I-want rebellion had tainted his own life to the point that he was powerless; moreover, he became faithless to the point that he thought that Elisha was also powerless. He had lost faith not only in God but also in God's man. Those who live by taking what is not theirs to take soon forget that God can give what is His to give.

I-Want-What-I-Want Lawlessness

Second Kings 5 gives the story of Naaman's cleansing, and when Naaman came back clean from the river Jordan, he returned in near-speechless gratitude to Elisha to bestow upon him a blessing. It was Naaman's desire to show appreciation for the wonderful miracle of his restored health by giving Elisha a present. Since he was captain of the entire host of the king of Syria, he certainly had plenty to give, but Elisha said, "As the LORD liveth, before whom I stand, I will receive none. And he urged him to take it; but he refused" (vs. 16).

Gehazi was standing by, listening in on this conversation, so when Captain Naaman left, Gehazi followed him. In his thoughts, he said, "As the LORD liveth, I will run after him, and take somewhat of him" (vs. 20). Notice the word "take" is used here, just as the past tense of it was in the account of Achan. Gehazi overtook the entourage of the captain outside the city. After Naaman stopped his carriages, Gehazi produced a lawless lie about two sons of the prophets who had dropped by to see Elisha just after Naaman had left. He went on to claim that Elisha had sent him to get a talent of silver and two changes of garments for the alleged visitors. Naaman, grateful as he was, urged Gehazi to take two talents of silver and two changes of garments, which Gehazi greedily took and hid in his house.

I-Want-What-I-Want Uselessness

When Gehazi returned to Elisha's presence, Elisha asked, "Whence comest thou, Gehazi?" (vs. 25), to which Gehazi responded that he had not been anywhere. This lawless lie, however, came to Elisha just after God had told him about Gehazi's lawless lies to Naaman. Elisha then revealed the servant's double heart when he asked him,

"Went not mine heart with thee, when the man turned

*again from his chariot to meet thee? Is it a time to receive
money, and to receive garments, and oliveyards, and vineyards,
and sheep, and oxen, and menservants, and maidservants?*

*"The leprosy therefore of Naaman shall cleave unto
thee...And he went out from his presence a leper as white as
snow."*—Vss. 26, 27.

Gehazi, due to his sinful pilgrimage from carelessness to
powerlessness to faithlessness to lawlessness was now useless
to the prophet from that moment forth.

The Corinthian Church

If ever a church received a scathing rebuke from an apostle, it was the Corinthian church in the letter of I Corinthians
from Paul. Their carnality and worldliness showed up in
many ways, but their action of going "to law before the unjust,
and not before the saints" (6:1) was a blatant example of I-
want-what-I-want rebellion in the New Testament church.
The things the apostle Paul said about them in the next seven
verses revealed much.

I-Want-What-I-Want Worthlessness

The I-want-what-I-want rebel will fight over worthless
things. Paul asked the Corinthians, "Are ye unworthy to judge
the smallest matters?" (vs. 2). These lawsuits where one
believer in the Corinthian church was going to law before the
unbelievers against another believer were not important matters. These were what the Holy Spirit called the "smallest matters," things that didn't matter! This type of rebellion will fight
over the most worthless things all for the sake of taking what
is technically not one's own at all.

I-Want-What-I-Want Worldliness

Paul next confronted the Corinthians' worldliness. Citing
the fact that believers will judge angels, he sarcastically asked

if they were unfit to judge things of this life! The I-want-what-I-want rebellion of the Corinthian church involved things that had no eternal bearing, things that were temporal and therefore temporary. Rebels are prone to enlarge the significance of the things of this life, creating tempests where God has placed a breeze.

I-Want-What-I-Want Wantonness

The comments of the apostle Paul were spoken to the shame of the Corinthian believers who should have known better. Their rebellion took them to greater and greater degrees of sinning one against another in the sight of the watching world. Rather than testifying to the world by their love for each other, the carnal Christians at Corinth were conducting themselves such that Paul had to rebuke them by saying, "There is utterly a fault among you, because ye go to law one with another" (vs. 7).

I-Want-What-I-Want Watchfulness

Last but not least, the Corinthians were watching out for themselves, as do all I-want-what-I-want rebels. The slogan "every man for himself" is the maxim by which these rebels operate. Paul asked them, "Why do ye not rather take wrong? why do ye not rather suffer yourselves to be defrauded?" (vs. 7). These two questions would have been meaningless had they been watching out for each other and making mature, spiritual decisions among themselves. Instead, each rebel was watching out for his own rights, his own possessions, his own territory. Instead of watching out for the name of Jesus Christ, the church of Jesus Christ and the testimony of Jesus Christ, they were concerned about self.

One preacher has wisely said that there is nothing as small as a rebel wrapped up in himself. The Corinthians were I-want-what-I-want rebels whose focus was getting what they wanted, regardless of the negative outcome upon others. "Nay, ye do wrong, and defraud, and that your brethren" (vs. 8) was Paul's Holy Spirit-inspired conclusion to the matter.

Illustration

A well-to-do Christian couple noted on more than one occasion that their daughter was wearing clothes which they did not remember purchasing. Whenever they would approach her, she would say that her outfit was a gift from a friend or something she won at the youth outing. Her parents were put off in this manner for a short time, but their suspicions were confirmed the day they were called by a security agent from a department store in the nearby mall. Their daughter had been caught shoplifting. The parents went together to the store, and after all the protocol, the father asked his daughter, "Why did you do this, Honey? You know we would buy you anything you need."

To this she glibly replied, "I wanted to. I just wanted some new things. I didn't want to bother you. I just wanted some new things." Four times in four sentences, the father noted she used a form of the word *wanted*.

The Rule the Righteous Live By

Contentment With Possessions

Chapter 9 closes with a treatment of contentment with position; this chapter closes with the concept of contentment regarding possessions. The righteous live by the rule of letting their "conversation be without covetousness; and [being] content with such things as [they] have: for he hath said, I will never leave thee, nor forsake thee" (Heb. 13:5). Knowing that they have God Himself as an ever abiding, personal God and Saviour, the righteous feel less stress to amass and attain in the realm of material things. Again, the righteous believers are told, "Lay not up for yourselves treasures upon earth...But lay up for yourselves treasures in heaven...For where your treasure is, there will your heart be also" (Matt. 6:19–21).

Two rather lengthy passages, Philippians 4:10–19 and I Timothy 6:6–19, serve as the gateposts through which the I-want-what-I-want rebel must pass if he is to leave his covetousness behind and enter into the blessed contentment of the righteous. In the Philippians passage, the apostle Paul writes of *learning contentment* with possessions. In the portion addressed to Timothy, he speaks of *living out* one's contentment with possessions. Since the learning precedes the living out, the Philippians passages will be considered first.

In Philippians, Paul's learning occurred in three steps, each beginning with the word "not." First, he said, "Not that I speak in respect of want: for I have learned, in whatsoever state I am, therewith to be content" (vs. 11). Here, he expressed that he had learned the righteous rule of contentment with possessions by seeing God's supply in *fluctuating circumstances.* Paul had learned not only through *abundance and fullness* but also through *abasement and famine* that he could do all the things he was supposed to do through Christ. Since he could still serve Christ regardless of his material status, he was content.

Second, Paul said, "Notwithstanding ye have well done, that ye did communicate with my affliction" (vs. 14). This "not" (*not*withstanding) showed that Paul had learned the righteous rule of contentment with possessions by observing God's supply through *faithful churches.* Even when he had only the Philippian church helping him when he first went to Macedonia (vs. 15), God had met the need. And it is certain that the Philippians were a faithful church, because, even though Paul's time in Thessalonica had included only three Sabbath days (Acts 17:2), they sent two separate gifts to him there in that time (Phil. 4:16).

Third, the apostle stated, "Not because I desire a gift: but I desire fruit that may abound to your account" (vs. 17). In this, he was relating that he learned the righteous rule of contentment with possessions by accepting God's supply as a *fruit-bearing contribution*. What the Philippians gave Paul was simply their investment in him so that they could "reap that whereon [they] bestowed no labour" (John 4:38). Paul had learned that the Philippians' gifts to him—or any church's gifts, for that matter—were not for him to waste on frivolities of his own desire. Rather, those gifts enabled those churches to enter into his labours and reap crowns and souls through him.

Any righteous believer who will learn like Paul did will be content with his possessions. He will not be an I-want-what-I-want rebel like Achan or Gehazi who covets and steals and hides his loot. Instead, he will live by the rule of contentment with his possessions because God is faithful all the time.

The other "gatepost," I Timothy 6:6–19, addresses the living out of the contentment that has been learned. Any righteous believer who has learned contentment with his possessions demonstrates it in one of two ways: if he is not rich, he still maintains his godliness; and if he is rich, he distributes and communicates those riches. These two divisions of I Timothy 6 are recognizeable by the phrases "But they that will be rich" (vs. 9), and, "Charge them that are rich" (vs. 17).

Those poorer believers who live out the righteous rule of contentment with their possessions are godly souls who realize that they brought nothing into the world and who are grateful for the meeting of life's basic needs. They do not go after this world's idle riches to the point of pursuing temptations and falling into snares and satisfying lusts and drowning in sin. They do not love money to the degree that they will depart from the faith and reap the sorrows of this world.

Instead, they maintain their "righteousness, godliness, faith, love, patience, meekness" (vs. 11). These righteous ones "fight the good fight of faith" (vs. 12), putting their energies into God's work, not their own wealth.

Richer believers who live out the righteous rule of contentment with possessions are not "highminded, nor [do they] trust in uncertain riches, but in the living God" (vs. 17). They prove this by doing good works with their money, by distributing their monies in substantial amounts to the servants of the Lord who are doing God's ministry, and by willingly communicating their profits with those who preach and teach. Truly, the ministry of Paul might have been even more fruitful if the wealthy Corinthian church (I Cor. 4:8) had been willing to invest in him and not spend their wealth suing for each other's wealth.

The righteous learn the rule of contentment with their possessions, and then they live by that rule. Without regard for amount of possession, they focus upon *frugality in the difficult times, generosity in the bountiful times* and *holiness of character at all times.*

15
The Anything-but-God Rule

"The wicked, through the pride of his countenance, will not seek after God: God is not in all his thoughts."

"The LORD knoweth the thoughts of man, that they are vanity."—Ps. 10:4; 94:11.

"They will not frame their doings to turn unto their God: for the spirit of whoredoms is in the midst of them, and they have not known the LORD."—Hos. 5:4.

"But they know not the thoughts of the LORD, neither understand they his counsel."—Mic. 4:12.

Certain rebels purposely and deliberately avoid any explanation of life experience that would exalt or extol God. The anything-but-God rebel may ascribe blessing to the benevolence of God or credit judgment to the righteous indignation of God. However, he will not turn to the God whom he may admit did the giving or taking. Regardless of the extremes to which anything-but-God rebels must go, they will avoid the obvious, straight-line-between-two-points answer that would lead them to acknowledge God as the one true God.

The Philistines

Anything-but-God Superstition

At the end of an ill-fated battle between the carnal Israelites and the wicked Philistines, "the ark of God was taken; and the two sons of Eli, Hophni and Phinehas, were slain" (I Sam. 4:11). The first thing the Philistines did with the ark was to carry it into their house of idols in Ashdod and set it next to the statue of their god, Dagon. After the gloating feasts of celebration so common in pagan societies, the people of Ashdod went to bed. Early the next morning when the people went to their idol temple, "behold, Dagon was fallen upon his face to the earth before the ark of the LORD" (5:3). Did the people of Ashdod reflect upon this obvious event? No. They simply picked up their god and put him back in his place, offered their empty prayers and went about their daily grind of senseless slavery to a dead god.

Early the next morning, those same worshipers returned to the shrine of Dagon. This time they discovered that "Dagon was fallen upon his face to the ground before the ark of the LORD; and the head of Dagon and both the palms of his hands were cut off upon the threshold; only the stump of Dagon was left to him" (vs. 4). Perhaps the first night's toppling of their idol could have been explained away as a natural phenomenon such as an earthquake tremor, but how did the Philistines explain that two mornings in a row their idol was face down before the ark of the covenant of the Lord of hosts? How did they respond to the fact that their false god's head and hands were severed?

Did the Philistines stop and ponder that their god was so impotent that they themselves had to pick him up and stand him back where he belonged? Did the Philistines reflect upon the obvious power of the God of the ark over the paltry ineptitude of Dagon? Did the pagan priests stop their people and tell them that they needed to forsake their incapable god and seek the God that could smash their icon before Himself? Did the rulers of Ashdod send to the elders of Gath, Ekron, Askelon and Gaza, the four other chief cities of the Philistines, and consult them regarding the pursuit of Jehovah God? The answer to these questions and a dozen others that could logically be asked is a resounding "no!" The anything-but-God rebels of Ashdod responded by making a new stipulation for all the worshipers of Dagon. From that day on, no priest or worshiper that entered the temple of Dagon could "tread on the threshold of Dagon in Ashdod" (vs. 5). That was all. Dagon was still their god, but they decided not to let their feet touch the threshold where his hands and head had lain after God knocked him out.

Because the rebellious people and their corrupt priests and foolish prophets did not wake up and smell the coffee, God stepped into their routine in greater power, and, with a heavy hand, He struck the city of Ashdod with a plague of emerods and destroyed many of the residents of that city. Did the survivors humble themselves before God? Did it occur to these anything-but-God rebels to seek and serve the God who was powerful enough to twice throw down their image and follow that up with a visitation of a plague? No. Instead, they gathered their confused lords in a conference where they determined that God was indeed heavily displeased with them and with Dagon, but their conclusion was merely to send the ark to Gath. On their part, there was no move whatsoever to transfer their allegiance and devotion to the greater God.

God was not any weaker in Gath than He had been in Ashdod. The emerods hit there too, so the foolish pagans sent the ark to Ekron where the citizens had heard enough at least to be afraid. They "cried out, saying, They have brought about the ark of the God of Israel to us, to slay us and our people" (vs. 10). The Philistines in Ekron had enough sense to realize that the God of the ark was the one afflicting them and destroying them, but their superstition compelled them not to seek Him. Anything-but-God rebels will always find another way to deal with the situation. And they did.

This time, the shortsighted priests and ill-guided diviners counseled their hapless subjects to fashion five golden mice and five golden emerods and put them into a coffer. Then, the people were instructed to place the coffer and the ark onto a cart, tie two milk cows to the cart and send them away. If the cows took the ark toward Beth-shemesh and the land of Israel, then they would agree that God had actually done the miracles against them. If the cows did not go toward Israel, they could conclude that the entire fiasco was a fluke.

The cows did head toward Beth-shemesh. Did that cause this nation of superstitious, anything-but-God worshipers to go back home, smash down their shrines to Dagon and seek Jehovah? Did that lead to their anything-but-God priests rending their garments and destroying their instruments of necromancy and witchcraft? No. The Philistines went right on devoting themselves to Dagon, following a god who could not stand up, a god who could not keep himself together, a god who could not resist disease, a god who could not defy destruction, a god who could not help them. Anything-but-God rebels will engage in the most ludicrous of religious customs and encumber themselves with all manner of superstitious beliefs, but they will not seek Almighty God.

The Servants of King Benhadad

Anything-but-God Statistics

First Kings 20 gives the story of the two major battles between the forces of Benhadad, king of Syria, and Ahab, king of Israel, in which the Israelites, though outnumbered by wide margins, brutally defeated the Syrians. The statistics in these battles were overwhelmingly embarrassing to the well-trained, world-class soldiers of Syria, but never did it occur to them to let Jehovah the true God into their minds and hearts. Instead, these anything-but-God rebels found *better* ways to explain why they were so crushingly defeated.

Before the first battle, Benhadad sent messengers to Ahab telling him that all Ahab's silver, gold, wives and children would soon be the possession of the Syrians; to this Ahab consented. The next messengers told Ahab that Benhadad would send servants to take those things they wanted from his house; to this Ahab gave no consent. This refusal on Ahab's part was the ancient Middle Eastern equivalent of a declaration of war. Benhadad was angered, and he swore by his gods that there would be more captive Israelites following him than there were handfuls of dust in Samaria! To this presumptuous boast, Ahab sent back a message that, incidentally, is the only wise thing preserved in Scripture from the mouth of Ahab. He told Benhadad, "Let not him that girdeth on his harness boast himself as he that putteth it off" (I Kings 20:11).

This message arrived at Benhadad's headquarters as he and his confederacy of kings were drinking, and Benhadad gave the command for the armies to be set in array. Simultaneously, a prophet of God assured Ahab of victory if he would send forth the Israelite army under the authority of the princes of the provinces. Although Ahab was no follower of Jehovah, Elijah had just executed all his prophets of Baal, so Ahab had no one else to consult. He listened to the prophet of God, and at noon, he attacked the Syrians while Benhadad and his fellow kings were drinking themselves drunk. In their inebriated state, Benhadad and his cartel had such impaired judgment that "the king of Israel...smote the horses and chariots, and slew the Syrians with a great slaughter" (vs. 21).

The prophet of God came again to Ahab after that battle and told him to strengthen his forces and get prepared because the Syrians would regroup and attack again. It was at this moment that the anything-but-God rebellion of the Syrian idol worshipers came to the surface. While the prophet of Jehovah God was advising Ahab to get ready for a Syrian resurgence, the Syrians were licking their wounds and explaining why the statistics of the battle had been as they were. "Their gods are gods of the hills; therefore they were stronger than we; but let us fight against them in the plain, and surely we shall be stronger than they," they reasoned (vs. 23). The Syrians then numbered an army man for man and chariot for chariot so that they would once again outnumber Israel by the same proportion as before. So lopsided were the two armies at the second battle that the writer of Kings said, "The children of Israel pitched before them like two little flocks of kids; but the Syrians filled the country" (vs. 27).

Upon this scene of seeming hopelessness, the man of God returned to tell Ahab that because the Syrians used any-thing-but-God reasoning to account for the statistics of their disastrous defeat in the hills in the first battle, God would also deliver Syria into Ahab's hands in the battle in the plains. The man of God then told Ahab that this victory (along with the first one) was designed to teach Ahab that Jehovah was the true and living Lord.

The anything-but-God rebels of Syria and the surrounding nations waited seven days in the plain, and in the seventh day, the armies charged one another. Israel was shockingly victorious, slaying one hundred thousand footmen that first day. Those who escaped fled to the city of Aphek, and twenty-seven thousand more died when a city wall collapsed upon them.

Would it not seem logical as well as spiritually sensible for the Syrians to take a long hard look at their back-to-back humiliating defeats and admit that there must have been some power other than stone gods and wooden images behind Israel's otherwise impossible victories? It would have been logical and spiritually sensible, but anything-but-God rebels are anything but logical and anything but spiritually sensible! God simply does not figure into their statistical equations.

The story continues with Ahab foolishly sparing Benhadad and then, for political expediency, calling him his brother. Remarkably, there is no record of Benhadad or any of the Syrian survivors or Ahab embracing Jehovah as Lord. God's entire purpose in bringing such astounding victories out of such impossible circumstances had been to show Ahab and everyone else that He really is God and Lord. The biblical narrative continues with Benhadad going back to Syria as a defeated anything-but-God rebel, with Ahab moving ever so much closer to his own demise, also as an anything-but-God rebel, and with the two nations of Israel and Syria still worshiping their false gods.

The Moabites

Anything-but-God Sacrifice

In the glorious days of Elisha's ministry, Mesha, king of Moab, decided to stop sending his annual rendering of one hundred thousand lambs and one hundred thousand rams with their wool to King Jehoram of Israel (II Kings 3:4). This sudden deficit to Israel's economy angered Jehoram, so he orchestrated an alliance between himself and King Jehoshaphat of Judah and the king of Edom. By means of this league of nations, Jehoram hoped to outnumber, attack and defeat Mesha, the Moabite king, so he could regain the economic benefits that had been temporarily withheld.

Even though God would not look upon Jehoram of Israel

or upon the king of Edom, God did condescend to intervene for this unholy coalition based strictly upon the presence of the righteous king Jehoshaphat. Elisha the prophet was God's mouthpiece to give the counsel. Where they had encamped, the soldiers of Judah, Israel and Edom were to dig the valley full of ditches and then offer their offering the following morning (vss. 16–20).

When the offering was offered the next day, God sent water to fill the ditches. From the other side of the valley, with the brilliant red morning sun shining upon the water with which God had miraculously filled the ditches, Mesha and his Moabite forces saw what they supposed to be blood. They concluded, "The kings are surely slain, and they have smitten one another: now therefore, Moab, to the spoil" (vss. 22, 23). They charged vulnerably right into the jaws of the waiting coalition soldiers who smote them, chased them, beat down their cities, marred their land, stopped their wells and felled their good trees (vss. 24, 25).

When Mesha finally perceived what was happening, he made a final, futile effort with seven hundred of his best soldiers in an effort to break through the lines and capture the king of Edom, but he could not. Did this anything-but-God rebel wave the white flag, call a retreat and surrender? Did he then humble himself before Jehoshaphat and beg for the mercy of the God who had humiliated him so badly? No. Instead, "he took his eldest son that should have reigned in his stead, and offered him for a burnt-offering upon the wall. And there was great indignation against Israel" (vss. 26, 27).

How simple it would have been for Mesha to realize that God had fooled him with the red water, that God had foiled his plans with something as simple as the reddish reflection of the sun! Instead, in an effort to appease Chemosh, his god, and merit enough of his favor to be granted a victory, he murderously sacrificed his own son in a show of anything-but-God rebellion. Anything-but-God rebels will give up anything—anything, that is, except their blind allegiance to their pseudo-gods. They will do anything except approach the true God.

Belshazzar

Anything-but-God Segregation

At the end of his life, the old emperor Nebuchadnezzar repented toward God and believed in Jehovah, but not until after he had been soundly embarrassed at the dedication of his ninety-foot image in the plains of Dura and sorely chastened by seven years of humiliating insanity. After the death of Nebuchadnezzar, his son and then his grandson by the name of Belshazzar reigned in his stead. This Belshazzar was an anything-but-God rebel whose revelry, debauchery and blasphemy topped that of his forebears and brought him to a precipitous and ignominious end. Part of Belshazzar's evil was his practical banishment of Daniel from public affairs. This wicked rebel segregated God's mighty prophet from all position of influence and relegated him to exile status to avoid his ministry.

When the sun arose upon the final day of Belshazzar's earthly life, he had no clue how foreboding that sunrise was. He and his top chamberlains orchestrated a grand and gala event honoring a thousand of his lords (Dan. 5). The celebrations had commenced, and as the lascivious revelings increased in magnitude, suddenly Belshazzar hit upon a plan. He commanded his servants to bring from the royal treasure house the golden and silver vessels which his grandfather Nebuchadnezzar had confiscated from the house of God when he plundered Jerusalem nearly seven decades earlier. Into those once-consecrated holy vessels, he poured the wine of drunkenness, and as those mindless souls sipped from the cups and flasks of the ancient Levitical priesthood, the God who had once sanctified those vessels with His own Shekinah glory decided it was time to pay Belshazzar a short visit.

Without any announcement or warning, "in the same hour came forth fingers of a man's hand, and wrote over against the candlestick upon the plaister of the wall of the king's palace" (vs. 5). Belshazzar was horror-stricken; his facial features strained at the mystery of it, and his knees rattled one against the other in an agonizing fear (vs. 6). Upon regaining his composure, he immediately summoned "the astrologers, the Chaldeans, and the soothsayers" (vs. 7), announcing to them that whichever of them could read and interpret the handwriting on the wall would be given royal apparel and made the third ruler in the kingdom. Belshazzar's wise men could no more read this writing than could his grandfather's wizards interpret dreams, but this anything-but-God rebel did not call in Daniel.

From the text of Daniel 5, it is obvious that Belshazzar had so long segregated Daniel to the outskirts of his kingly function that he had altogether forgotten that Daniel even existed! In fact, it was Belshazzar's wife who came to the rescue, reminding him that there was in his kingdom a man in whom resided the Spirit of God and who had read mysteries for Nebuchadnezzar. Once Daniel was called, he addressed the anything-but-God rebel who had segregated him from all public or private persuasion. Daniel reminded Belshazzar about his grandfather's kingdom, of the pride that hardened his heart, and of the years during which he had been insane. Then he said to Belshazzar, "And thou his son, O Belshazzar, hast not humbled thine heart, though thou knewest all this; But hast lifted up thyself against the Lord of heaven" (vss. 22, 23). In essence, he was declaring that Belshazzar was an anything-but-God rebel who would do anything but repent, anything but turn to God. Then he read the message that God had numbered Belshazzar's kingdom and finished it, had weighed him personally and found him wanting, and had divided his kingdom and given it to the Medes and the Persians. The entire party ended abruptly, and "in that night was Belshazzar the king of the Chaldeans slain" (vs. 30).

Knowing all that had befallen his grandfather, Belshazzar could have chosen to honor Jehovah. Having perfect awareness of the ability of God to raise up and put down, he could have elected to follow the God of Daniel. Having at his disposal the great prophet Daniel, he could have availed himself of the prophet's wisdom. Instead, he was an anything-but-God rebel who ignored the entire working of God in his grandfather, who scoffed at his grandfather's late-life testimony regarding the God of Daniel, who segregated Daniel from public service so he would not have him as a daily presence in the court, who still consulted with the false and useless astrologers of Chaldean occultism, and who bent over backward to desecrate all memory of the true God. To the last minute that his soul was upon earth, he did anything and everything to avoid God altogether.

The Chief Priests and Sadducees: Annas, Caiaphas, John and Alexander

Anything-but-God Stubbornness

In the third chapter of Acts, the apostles Peter and John encountered a man who was asking alms at the gate Beautiful of the temple. This man, above forty years of age, had a congenital birth defect that left him unable to walk. Each day, he was carried to this location where he could obtain meager subsistence. On the way to prayer, the two apostles observed him, and Peter told him, "Silver and gold have I none; but such as I have give I thee: In the name of Jesus Christ of Nazareth rise up and walk" (vs. 6). So immediately that it was attributable only to God, he was completely healed and was seen walking and leaping about, praising God for the miracle of restoration he had just experienced.

As the people, some of whom had seen him every day of their lives lying as a beggar at the gate, milled about and gawked at this man, Peter took further opportunity to preach of Jesus, the resurrected Saviour whose power it was that had made the man to walk. He did not hedge one bit, but he addressed their crucifixion of the Lord Christ, announcing that their rulers were ignorant, showing that the entire event was fulfillment of prophecy, and teaching that Christ's sacrifice and resurrection were for their blessing and forgiveness.

Upon this scene of miracle and message came a posse of anything-but-God rebels, "the priests, and the captain of the temple, and the Sadducees...Being grieved that they taught the people, and preached through Jesus the resurrection from the dead" (4:1, 2). Because it was evening, these self-exalted authorities cast Peter and John into the prison until the following morning, whereupon they brought them forth to cross-examine them with the impertinent question, "By what power, or by what name, have ye done this?" (vs. 7). Ever the spiritual opportunist, Peter again spoke in the fullness of the Spirit of God and preached a mighty sermon to these anything-but-God rebels who were so piously judging them.

In the following verses of Acts 4, several things occurred which should have been indicators to these stubborn, any-thing-but-God rebels that they were witnessing an anything-but-normal situation! First, the Sadducees "saw the boldness of Peter and John, and perceived that they were unlearned and ignorant men...and...took knowledge of them, that they had been with Jesus" (vs. 13). The very fact that the previous day Peter had preached a message that resulted in the saving faith of five thousand Jews and that Peter could preach a second masterful message that so closely resembled the preaching style of the Master Himself should have broken through the facade of these Sadducees' religiosity, but in true form, they stubbornly refused to admit that this was God at work.

Next, they beheld "the man which was healed standing with them" (vs. 14). As if the mighty messages were not enough, the proof of the apostles' power and effectiveness stood beside them and all around them. Undoubtedly, many of those converted the previous day were in the audience, but most amazing of all, there stood the man who had been lame from his mother's womb! Did these stubborn anything-but-God rebels go aside into private counsel and agree to surrender and admit that God had used the apostles and that God was at work through someone other than themselves? Oh, they went aside into private counsel to be sure, but that counsel was not for the purpose of acknowledging God. Instead, their agreed-upon modus operandi was to "straitly threaten them [to] speak henceforth to no man in this name [and to command] them not to speak at all nor teach in the name of Jesus" (vss. 17, 18).

Peter would not be silenced by a politico-religious muzzle, so he responded with what has become a standby of fundamentalism: "Whether it be right in the sight of God to hearken unto you more than unto God, judge ye. For we cannot but speak the things which we have seen and heard" (vss. 19, 20). Seeing no further action that they could take against them, and realizing that the assembled crowd was on the apostles' side, the Sadducees threatened them once again and let them go.

The apostles immediately went to the believers, reported the entire situation to them, and organized a praise and prayer meeting that resulted in such Holy Spirit empowerment that they spoke with renewed boldness in their public ministry. This enhanced and recharged group of apostles did not long stay out of the limelight—nor out of prison. Their resurfacing in Jerusalem merely days after having been so strictly threatened alarmed the Sadducees who again had them jailed. This time, the angel of the Lord released them, and when the Sadducees sent for them, the jailors said, "The prison truly found we shut with all safety, and the keepers standing without before the doors: but when we had opened, we found no man within" (5:23).

Again, the Lord was giving these stubborn anything-but-God rebels an opportunity to repent of their stubbornness and acknowledge that the apostles were of God. Again, these stubborn anything-but-God rebels decided not to do anything of the sort. When word came that Peter and the others were standing in the temple preaching and teaching in the very name that the Sadducees had prohibited, the chief captain of the temple went with some of his officers and "brought them without violence: for they feared the people, lest they should have been stoned" (vs. 26).

When Peter and his fellows were arraigned before the Sadducees for the second time, the high priest asked "Did not we straitly command you that ye should not teach in this name? and, behold, ye have filled Jerusalem with your doctrine, and intend to bring this man's blood upon us" (vs. 28). Incidentally, it was "this man's blood" that they had just weeks before voluntarily taken upon themselves with their chanting, "His blood be on us, and on our children" (Matt. 27:25)! Peter again countered them with his famous words, "We ought to obey God rather than men" (Acts 5:29), and then he preached them another fiery sermon that cut them to the heart to the point that they determined to kill the apostles.

This time, it was not a Sadducee but a Pharisee (Gamaliel, teacher of Saul of Tarsus) who stood up and quelled the raging of the council. By his citing of others whose movements were boastful escapades that came to nothing, he persuaded the Sadducees to release the apostles, to leave them alone and wait to see if God would either allow their work to fizzle or promote it to the front lines. The Sadducees agreed to this, beat the apostles, further commanded them to silence and released them (vss. 34–40).

All of this back-and-forth conflict between the apostles and the Sadducees was fraught with opportunity for the Sadducees to admit that God was in their midst, that God was doing something, that God was really alive and active and productive. But like the liberals of any age, they were stubborn in their anything-but-God rebellion and refused to give credit to God. It is a question unanswered by Scripture how those anything-but-God rebels explained the boldness of Peter and John, the permanent healing of the lame man, the thousands of converts to Christianity, the joy of the apostles despite their troubles, and the continual thwarting of their efforts to squelch Christianity. What is known is that these Sadducees did not explain all these matters by saying that God was at work. Anything-but-God rebels just don't do that.

The Residents of Melita

Anything-but-God Simplicity

The apostle Paul encountered some superstitious, anything-but-God rebels on the isle of Melita after his third shipwreck. Having floated on ship boards or swum ashore, the two hundred seventy-six hunger-weakened, storm-battered souls huddled around a makeshift fire to counteract the effects of the bone-chilling sea waters and the cold rain. As Paul laid a bundle of sticks on the fire, a poisonous snake suddenly crawled out of those sticks to escape the intense heat and bit him on the hand.

"And when the barbarians saw the venomous beast hang on

his hand, they said among themselves, No doubt this man is a murderer, whom, though he hath escaped the sea, yet vengeance suffereth not to live.

"And he shook off the beast into the fire, and felt no harm.

"Howbeit they looked when he should have swollen, or fallen down dead suddenly: but after they had looked a great while, and saw no harm come to him, they changed their minds, and said that he was a god."—Acts 28:4–6.

The simplicity of anything-but-God rebels is aptly illustrated by the response of these islanders. If they had not ever heard Christ personally, they had heard of Him. If they had not personally heard the Gospel itself, they had unquestionably heard of it. If they had not yet heard Paul himself, they had heard of him. Their designation as barbarians does not mean that they were savages as much as it means they were not Greek-cultured, Greek-educated persons. They were simpleminded islanders, well-settled in their ages-old ignorances and fables.

Rather than accept that God had His hand upon their shipwrecked visitor, they first resorted to fatalism to explain the snakebite and then relied upon polytheism to explain Paul's obvious immunity to the snakebite. These people could have easily said, "This must be one of those Christians we have heard about," but then, anything-but-God rebels do not say that. They explain the obvious by intricate and convoluted reasonings rather than submit to the plain, beautiful teaching of the one true God and His Son, Jesus Christ. The Word of God details how these simple islanders lodged the shipwrecked passengers, experienced the healings of Paul in their midst, honored them all with many gifts, and after three months laded the new ship with what was needed, but there is no record of one of those anything-but-God souls believing in Jesus Christ.

Illustration

A Christian man who had faithfully served in a local church for about thirty years began to experience some disturbing and unexplainable physical symptoms. Upon seeking medical counsel and undergoing some preliminary testing, he was told news that no one wants to hear. "Sir," said the doctor in charge of his case, "you have inoperable, untreatable, malignant cancer in the fourth stage, and there is nothing we can do for you." On the way home, that man stopped at his pastor's house and told him the doctor's words. Then he said, "Pastor, there is something God can do for me." That pastor called six other area pastors, he, along with his church body, to come to a special meeting on a Friday evening. After the singing of many hymns and spiritual songs, the reading of several Scripture promises, and the observing of quiet moments of meditation, the six pastors anointed the ill man with oil in the name of the Lord. Then they prayed the prayer of faith, trusting God for healing. As the third pastor of the six was praying, the sick man felt movement inside him like what he thought a woman must feel when a baby moves in her womb. He immediately sensed strength and wholeness.

When the praying was done, he stood up and confidently declared that he knew he had been healed. He drove the next day to his doctor's office and declared the details of his healing to the doctor. Further medical testing revealed that the three large tumors and the several smaller ones had vanished. Blood work revealed the absolute absence of cancer cells in the man's body. As the man sat in the presence of the physician, he testified of Christ and of the power of God. The doctor said, "The mysterious disappearance of your tumors may be due to any number of factors, but God had nothing to do with it." He was an anything-but-God rebel covering an empty heart with a white coat.

The Rule That the Righteous Live By

Omnipotence

Rather than use anything-but-God reasoning, the righteous freely and joyfully admit that God is in and upon and above everything. When ordinary events of life unfold, the righteous see the omnipotent, sovereign, preeminent hand of God, acknowledging that "in him we live, and move, and have our being" (Acts 17:28). When God sends an out-of-the-ordinary situation into the life of a Christian, the righteous child of God willingly and readily acknowledges, "He is thy praise, and he is thy God, that hath done for thee these great...things, which thine eyes have seen" (Deut. 10:21). And when the truly extraordinary occurs, he humbles himself in thanksgiving and then exalts Christ in his declarations: "What hath God wrought!" (Num. 23:23) and, "Our God is in the heavens: he hath done whatsoever he hath pleased" (Ps. 115:3).

It is incumbent upon the righteous believer in Christ to do what Jesus commanded the demoniac of Gadara to do after the devils were cast out: "Return to thine own house, and shew how great things God hath done unto thee" (Luke 8:39). That man did go his way, and he did publish abroad the wonderful works of God such that his entire city heard and knew. The psalmist four times adjured believers, "Oh that men would praise the LORD for his goodness, and for his wonderful works to the children of men!" (Ps. 107:8, 15, 21, 31). If believers want to avoid being anything-but-God rebels, they must be all-about-God righteous servants, telling anyone and everyone about the goodness of God in all the matters of life, big and small, significant and insignificant, known and unknown.

Israel "forgat God their saviour, which had done great things in Egypt" (106:21). The righteous are the type of people who freely admit that God is involved in every detail of life, exclaiming, "Thy righteousness also, O God, is very high, who hast done great things: O God, who is like unto thee!" (71:19), and declaring to those around them, "The LORD hath done great things for us; whereof we are glad" (126:3).

16
The Be-Yourself Rule

"And he said to them all, If any man will come after me, let him deny himself, and take up his cross daily, and follow me.

"For whosoever will save his life shall lose it: but whosoever will lose his life for my sake, the same shall save it.

"For what is a man advantaged, if he gain the whole world, and lose himself, or be cast away?

"For whosoever shall be ashamed of me and of my words, of him shall the Son of man be ashamed, when he shall come in his own glory, and in his Father's, and of the holy angels."—Luke 9:23–26.

"Verily, verily, I say unto you, Except a corn of wheat fall into the ground and die, it abideth alone: but if it die, it bringeth forth much fruit.

"He that loveth his life shall lose it; and he that hateth his life in this world shall keep it unto life eternal."—John 12:24, 25.

The Lord Jesus Christ artfully explained the difference between a man's being himself in self-living and a man's being himself in God-living. The cited passages along with several parallels in the Gospels all indicate that submission to God involves denying or losing the self-life, while rebellion includes the attempt to keep or find or save one's self-life. The goal of the be-yourself rebel is to accomplish all that is within his human grasp to the complete neglect of what God created and called him to be and do. He is like the self-styled man in a Dr. Seuss poem:

> Today you are you;
> That is truer than true.
> There is no one alive
> Who is youer than you.

It is the position of this rebel that he is free and even obligated to be himself. After all, did not God create us all as individuals? Be-yourself rebels' piety on such subjects would be nearly plausible were it not so evident from their lifestyles that they could hardly care less for the Creator God's design for their lives as a whole or His desires for their lives on a daily basis.

Fundamental to the be-yourself rebel is the zealous resistance to conformity to Christ; however, there is no resistance on the part of this rebel to *conform* to the world, *cave* to the flesh and *cater* to the Devil! In all their efforts to convince the church they are simply being who they are, they demonstrate that they are really being who the world and the flesh are. They are not as individual as they claim to be; they are clones of a godless world system whose adherents think, look, dress, talk and act alike.

Samson

In seventy-one verses, Judges 14–16 gives over forty self-references by Samson. His entire focus, his whole impetus in life, was himself. Had Samson truly been the distinct individual God had created and called him to be, he would have been "a Nazarite unto God from the womb" and he would have done more than just "begin to deliver Israel out of the hand of the Philistines" (13:5); he would have consummated that task. Samson would have been a Nazarite and a judge with the potential to have been as great a character and hero of faith as

Samuel, who, though he was not called a Nazarite, seems from I Samuel 1:11 to have been one, making him the only other Nazarite judge in Scripture.

He could have been more mightily used by the Lord had he not chosen to be himself instead of the person God ordained him to be. Samson's Spirit-empowered accomplishments did not include bringing his fellow Hebrews back to God or introducing the neighboring nations to Him. Instead, once "the Spirit of the LORD began to move him at times in the camp of Dan between Zorah and Eshtaol" (vs. 25), he exploited the Spirit's power to the advantage of his untamed lusts. Such amazing displays of fleshly accomplishment as capturing three hundred foxes or carrying the city gates and posts to the top of a hill before Hebron or breaking ropes as though they were threads had no spiritual or eternal consequence that bettered his nation, his family or even his own life. Someone has said that his life can be outlined in the following way:

I. Living by Righteousness (chapter 13)

II. Living by Rashness (chapter 14)

III. Living by Reaction (chapter 15)

IV. Living by Regrets (chapter 16)

His pathetic exit from life is a self-emphasizing prayer of thirty-three words (16:28) in which he mentions God twice and himself six times! That prayer was followed by the deaths of about three thousand Philistines, more than he had slain in his lifetime. That means that he killed fewer than six thousand in his twenty-year judgeship, and one thousand of those came on one occasion (15:15). If the Spirit could so empower him for such an achievement on one day, then his accomplishments over two decades should have been much more, but he was squandering his time and talents, as well as the Spirit's filling, on his own passions.

Be-Yourself Pleasures

Samson first exemplified his rebellion with be-yourself pleasures. When he went down to Timnath and saw a sensually beautiful Philistine girl, he told his parents about her and "said unto his father, Get her for me; for she pleaseth me well" (14:3). Rather than seek the spiritual pleasures available to him as a Nazarite, he pursued the baser pleasures of rebellious carnality. The statement that says "his father and his mother knew not that it was of the LORD, that he sought an occasion against the Philistines" (vs. 4) is not an expression of God's approval. And his parents clearly did not like the arrangement either, as the previous verse proves. God assuredly would not bless that union, for the rule was for Israelites in general to remain separate from the heathen around them. How much more would that apply to a Nazarite?

What *was* "of the LORD" was the judgment that was to come on the oppressing Philistines; what *was not* of the Lord was the method Samson employed. Samson fulfilled the "what" of God's will, but not the "how." God never authorized Samson to pursue his vulgar passions; however, He did release him to those base be-yourself pleasures. Consequently, the one born to be a Nazarite judge completely ignored his parents' warnings against marriage to an uncircumcised Philistine and his God's commands to the same effect.

Be-Yourself Precipitancy

Samson next bore witness of be-yourself rebellion when he precipitously decided to defile his Nazarite vow. Perhaps he was angry because he had met with resistance from his parents regarding the Philistine woman from Timnath. Without discretion, he went to Timnath and took the path through the vineyards where he likely ate grapes, thus defiling one tenet of his Nazarite separation.

There a lion (portraying the Devil) threatened him, and Samson killed the lion barehanded. After he spent a carnally pleasing time with the Philistine girl, he returned home. When he was going to take his bride, he took the same route and decided to go and see the dead lion. He found that bees had swarmed in and had begun to make honey in a hollow chamber of the decaying carcass, and he reached his hand into the bees' nest and scooped out honey and ate it, although a Nazarite was not to touch something that was dead.

In foolish carelessness, he quickly defiled his Nazarite vow on two of its three counts. Rebellion often takes sudden turns. Be-yourself rebels are widely known for *precipitous decisions* that bring *permanent defilement*. Besides not cutting his hair, Samson was never to be involved with any fruit of the vine or any dead carcass. With reckless indifference toward his vow, he contaminated his testimony and prostituted his purity. The spiritual heritage which he had possessed since birth was gone because he precipitously discarded it. This avoidable loss all issued out of unguarded self-indulgence.

Be-Yourself Privacy

Once Samson had discovered that communicating his rebellious wants to his parents brought their rebukes, and after he had broken two of the three conditions of his Nazarite vow, he engaged in be-yourself privacy. He opted not to tell his parents about his side trip into the vineyard, his slaying of the lion and his later contact with the decaying remains. Judges 14:6 says, "He told not his father or his mother what he had done," and verses 9 and 16 also reveal him withholding pertinent information from his parents.

Samson was an adult with God's calling upon his life, and that would seem to release him somewhat from his parents' oversight. However, there is no place where God excuses or condones any child's sinful secrecy from his parents. Secret faults are to be *cleansed,* not *closeted.* Secret sins are to be *confessed,* not *confined.* Any sin in a child that adversely affects the holy heritage that his parents have labored to pass on should be revealed to those parents so that restitution and restoration can ensue. Because Samson was not grown up in his spirit and soul, his actions were immature and ungodly. This pattern of secretive behavior gave Samson a mood of uninhibited license through the absence of any possibility of his parents' cautions.

Be-Yourself Prowess

Samson and his father (and perhaps his mother) made a feast to celebrate the Philistine woman, and he married her. The Philistines supplied thirty companions to attend to Samson during the seven days of the marriage feast. Samson used this festive occasion to put forth a riddle about the honey in the carcass of the lion. The agreement was that if they could solve the riddle "out of the eater came forth meat, and out of the strong came forth sweetness" (vs. 14) in seven days' time, he would give them thirty sheets and thirty changes of garments. If they could not solve that riddle in the allotted time, they would give those prizes to him.

Samson most surely sensed and felt his defilement, and such people often want to show themselves better than others so they will feel good about themselves again. Perhaps this is why he developed the contest with the riddle. Samson knew they would never guess the riddle. Who could have known what he was alluding to or hinting at? He had been alone in the vineyard where he killed the lion. He had been alone again when he drew out the honey to eat. He had told no one. By this, he could show himself clever and smart and subtle. By the end of the week when they had not found out his riddle, he would feel superior and better than those lowly Philistines— even though he would still know inside that he was defiled.

What Samson did not anticipate was that his wife's people

would threaten her and her father with death by fire if she did not give them the answer. Nor did Samson anticipate that she would display such loyalty to her Philistine heritage—a degree of loyalty he should have manifested toward his God and his parents! She pressed him and cajoled him and teased him until he told her. Then she told them, they told him, and Samson's prowess balloon popped in the middle of the seventh day of the feast.

Be-Yourself Principles

The details of Samson's life next reveal his be-yourself principles. The deflating of his ego in front of the Philistines maddened him. Rather than take his lumps, he murdered thirty men and stole their sheets and garments to give to the thirty companions. Later, in an effort to have some fleshly comfort, he went to take his wife, but his father-in-law would not allow Samson to have her. The father-in-law told Samson he had given his wife to one of the friends, but that he could have her younger sister. To this, Samson reacted with fiery rage, capturing three hundred foxes, tying them tail-to-tail with firebrands and sending them into the Philistines' fields of standing corn. The Philistines' response was to burn Samson's wife and her father to death. Still not satisfied, Samson got even with them by smiting "them hip and thigh with a great slaughter" (Judg. 15:8). When Samson's countrymen confronted him for stirring up the ire of their Philistine overlords, he said, "As they did unto me, so have I done unto them" (vs. 11).

All this chaos and turmoil exhibited the thumb-sucking principles of a be-yourself rebel. Samson was not governed by God's truth, God's will or God's anything. He did what he did to get even. If he had to murder to get even, he murdered. If he had to destroy to get even, he destroyed. If he had to cause difficulty for his compatriots to get even, he caused difficulty. Whatever he needed to do to get even, he did it. The life principles of a be-yourself rebel are often connected to self-justifying vengeance.

Be-Yourself Poverty

The next incident in Samson's life involved the men of Judah. Because he had angered the Philistines, the men of Judah came to bind him so they could turn him over to the Philisitines. Samson agreed to this on condition that they would not attack him themselves. Once the men of Judah had thoroughly laced him up, they took him to the Philistines in Lehi. When the Philistines gave a loud shout, "the cords that were upon [Samson's] arms became as flax that was burnt with fire" (vs. 14), and "he found a new jawbone of an ass, and put forth his hand, and took it, and slew a thousand men therewith" (vs. 15). Despite Samson's touching a newly dead animal bone, God condescended and gave him victory.

At that moment, Samson demonstrated be-yourself poverty. After such a mighty moving of God, Samson simply threw away the jawbone by which God had wrought the deliverance! Samson's great exertion left him exhausted and athirst, and while he did not separate from the uncircumcised in his relationships, he did not want them to kill him. Between a rock and a hard place, he cried out to God, and God brought forth water out of that discarded jawbone. The poverty of be-yourself rebels is that they cannot appreciate the value of spiritual power or victory on the rare occasions when they have it, and, therefore, they cast away the "Ebenezer stone" of God's deliverance.

Be-Yourself Pitfall

From Lehi, Samson went to Gaza to a harlot. The Gazites fenced him in, but at midnight he went away with the "doors of the gate of the city, and the two posts...bar and all" (16:3) balanced upon his shoulders and carried them to the crest of a hill before Hebron. The crazed and intemperate lust of his be-yourself rebellion was about to turn him upon his own head and drown him in destruction and perdition. This happened in full when he met Delilah in the valley of Sorek.

All the selfish pleasures, all the precipitous decisions to do wrong, all the secretive privacy, all the empty prowess, all the vengeful principles, all the poverty of spiritual bankruptcy, and all the moral pitfalls finally came full circle. Delilah was the tool the Devil used to destroy Samson. He had ignored all the special provisions of his Nazarite vow except cutting his hair. He had frittered away all the unique power of his Nazarite vow on useless exploits. In Delilah's lap, all the selfish indulgence of be-yourself rebellion came to a tragic end.

In being himself, Samson was really being nothing. One must ask what spiritual blessing or military victory came as a result of his twenty-year judgeship. One must ask what national honor or personal advantage came as a result of his be-yourself rebellion against being a Nazarite. The answer is that there was precious little spiritual blessing, military victory, national honor or personal advantage. His mention in Hebrews 11 does indicate that he was a man of faith, but he subdued no kingdom, wrought almost no righteousness, obtained no promise, quenched no fire and turned to flight no alien armies. On the positive side, he did stop the mouth of a lion, albeit in disobedience; and he was often made strong out of weakness, but, alas, only to use that strength for his own sordid capers.

Samson's be-yourself rebellion left him blind and powerless in the pitfall of his own self-life, *grinding* in the prison house of the enemy camp, *groping* his way to the support post of the idol temple in tow of a little lad, and *groaning* in an ignominious death without ever having accomplished anything lasting or beneficial. Be-yourself rebellion never glorifies God, lifts the standard, raises the hopes or strengthens those dependent upon the rebel. To the contrary, be-yourself rebellion leaves holes of want and gaps of lack everywhere it is practiced. Samson departed this life having been nearly useless to God, despite starting out with the potential of being exceptionally useful.

Solomon

The be-yourself life has no value to God or man. Samson's be-yourself life displays the utter lack of meaningful value to God, while Solomon's be-yourself life shows the complete absence of meaningful value to the person living that be-yourself life. Reading the Book of Ecclesiastes with any degree of understanding leads quickly to the conclusion that the writer was not a fulfilled, satisfied soul. The lament of that book, "Vanity of vanities; all is vanity," is stated in one form or another more than a dozen times in just twelve chapters! The basic reason that Solomon was not fulfilled and that his life was of no value to himself is that he pursued his own best calculation of the be-yourself life to the exclusion of the life God had planned out for him.

Much of Ecclesiastes is written in the first person where Solomon employs the word "I" over eighty times in two hundred twenty-two verses, with *me, mine,* and *myself* appearing another few dozen times. This translates into a self-reference by Solomon on an average of more than once in every other verse in the book. Ecclesiastes is a book of the be-yourself life, a record proving that when all focus is upon oneself, the indulged individual is miserable! While it would be unwieldy in this chapter to identify every point of Solomon's life that showed the be-yourself rebellion, allow me to lay a foundation and then identify a few key aspects of this trait that Solomon's life so obviously portrayed.

Solomon had the potential to be greater than his father,

David. At Solomon's coronation, Benaiah, the son of Jehoiada, prayed the dedicatory prayer in which he said, "As the LORD hath been with my lord the king, even so be he with Solomon, and make his throne greater than the throne of my lord king David" (I Kings 1:37). After Solomon's establishment as king, God "appeared to Solomon in a dream by night: and God said, Ask what I shall give thee" (3:5). Solomon's answer displayed a wisdom far beyond his years: "Give...thy servant an under-standing heart to judge thy people" (vs. 9). God answered His new king,

> *"I have given thee a wise and an understanding heart; so that there was none like thee before thee, neither after thee shall any arise like unto thee.*
>
> *"And I have also given thee that which thou hast not asked, both riches, and honour: so that there shall not be any among the kings like unto thee all thy days.*
>
> *"And if thou wilt walk in my ways, to keep my statutes and my commandments, as thy father David did walk, then I will lengthen thy days."*—Vss. 12–14.

The promises of wisdom, understanding, riches and honor were unconditional. The covenant of lengthened days, however, was conditional upon Solomon's piety and holiness. The literal meaning of the lengthened days was that God would lengthen the days of Solomon's reign beyond the forty years of his father's reign—if Solomon would follow God as David followed God.

Upon such a glorious promise of increase and potential, Solomon began to reign and build. He took care of his father David's unfinished business with Adonijah, Joab and Shimei. He established himself through the judicious decision regarding the two harlots and the surviving infant (vss. 16–28). He built the temple, and the God of Heaven filled that temple with His Shekinah glory. He built his own houses and a great name and a mighty kingdom. God gave him peace and rest and security within the nation, such that he had "neither adversary nor evil occurrent" (5:4).

Be-Yourself Paradise

Solomon, however, began to become wealthier, using his immense cache of riches to aggrandize himself in the creation of an "earthly Eden," a be-yourself paradise. His annual revenue would translate as billions of dollars today. His artificers built lavishly ornate thrones and fashioned luxurious gold shields and drinking vessels such that silver was "nothing accounted of in the days of Solomon" (10:21). Since silver is representative of redemption, that statement reveals much. He imported exotic birds and animals. He received emissaries and ambassadors and kings and queens from other lands who came for no other reason than to admire him and his kingdom. The common astonishment among the visiting dignitaries was expressed by the queen of Sheba who said she did not believe what she had heard until she had seen it; her conclusion was, "The half was not told me" (vs. 7).

Be-Yourself Prodigality

Ecclesiastes, chapters 1 and 2, supplement the accounts of Solomon's life in I Kings and II Chronicles with their list of more of the grandiose plans and achievements of this ancient king. His prodigal bent was such that he taxed the people heavily to indulge his vast dreams and to bring his wants to reality. He had vineyards, gardens, orchards and pools upon his personal property. His servants and maidens were left unnumbered because there were so many waiting upon his whims and wishes. He owned large and small cattle in sizable herds. He collected trinkets and souvenirs from kingdoms near and far. He had musical and dramatic entertainment. Indeed, he said, "And whatsoever mine eyes desired I kept not from them, I withheld not my heart from any joy" (Eccles. 2:10).

Be-Yourself Profligacy

As is the case in nearly every instance of be-yourself rebellion, Solomon's be-yourself *prodigal extravagance* was followed by *profligate experience.* He engaged in the partying, drinking, reveling life. He married heathen women by the hundreds and had hundreds more concubines. Although these liaisons were mostly for political expediency, "his wives turned away his heart after other gods: and his heart was not perfect with the LORD his God, as was the heart of David his father" (I Kings 11:4). Such was his departure from God that five and one-half centuries later his be-yourself rebellion was still remembered: "Did not Solomon king of Israel sin by these things? yet among many nations was there no king like him, who was beloved of his God, and God made him king over all Israel: nevertheless even him did outlandish women cause to sin" (Neh. 13:26).

Be-Yourself Privation

While it may be difficult for anyone but the ultrarich to comprehend the luxurious splendor of Solomon's be-yourself life, what can be understood by all is that he had everything but happiness. In all his accumulation, all he could feel and experience was deprivation. He arrived at the destination where all be-yourself rebellion ultimately leads. He said, "I have seen all the works that are done under the sun; and, behold, all is vanity and vexation of spirit" (Eccles. 1:14). He concluded, "Therefore I hated life....Yea, I hated all my labour which I had taken under the sun" (2:17, 18). It is clear that he was unhappy, because happy people do not whine about vanity and vexation of spirit and pine about hating life!

Solomon lived for many years as the person he wanted to be at the expense of being the person God wanted him to be. Interestingly, God had unconditionally promised him all the riches and honor. He could have had those things and happiness too, *if* he had simply chosen to be God's man, not man's man. And had Solomon agreed to be God's king in God's will, he would have enjoyed all those temporal blessings rather than hating them. They would have provided him with precious happiness, not the privation of emptiness.

Illustration

Following a particular message in which a pastor focused on some specific sins from a particular passage of Scripture, a man approached him in the lobby. He said he wanted a private session with the pastor, and the pastor accommodated him right then. This man told the pastor that he had no right to preach against a person's sins, because each person is just being himself. He went on to state that just like a missionary is being himself, so a drug user is being himself. He concluded by stating that the one is no better or any different than the other in the eyes of a loving, accepting God. The man who was speaking to the pastor was known as a be-yourself rebel who was involved in illegal drug use and illicit immorality.

The Rule That the Righteous Live By

Transformation and Conformity

Fundamental to being the person God wants one to be rather than being oneself is knowing and doing the will of God. God saved each one of His saints so "that he no longer should live the rest of his time in the flesh to the lusts of men, but to the will of God" (I Pet. 4:2). Like David, the man after God's own heart (i.e. God's will), "served his own generation by the will of God" (Acts 13:36), so each righteous believer is obligated to serve his present generation that way. Scripture has given a specific way for every one of His saints to know the will of God for his own life.

First, the righteous believer must undergo metamorphosis, a complete transformation from the control of sin to the control of God's Spirit. Paul said,

> "I beseech you therefore, brethren, by the mercies of God, that ye present your bodies a living sacrifice, holy, acceptable unto God, which is your reasonable service.
>
> "And be not conformed to this world: but be ye transformed by the renewing of your mind, that ye may prove what is that good, and acceptable, and perfect, will of God."—Rom. 12:1, 2.

Each righteous saint who longs to be the person God wants him to be and not end up as a be-yourself rebel must meet three fundamental conditions: (1) willing presentation of the body, (2) godly sanctification of the will, and (3) spiritual transformation of the mind. Having met those conditions, the child of God has the Lord's promise of knowing without question the will of God for his personal life.

Once the will of God is known, the righteous will live by the rule of conformity—"not conformed to this world", but "conformed to the image of his Son" (8:29). In accomplishing this, the righteous must carefully and consistently purify and cleanse himself "with the washing of water by the word" (Eph. 5:26), "for this is the will of God, even your sanctification" (I Thess. 4:3). God desires and uses only clean vessels. The believer who finds daily cleansing in the Scripture (John 15:3; 17:17) and under the blood (I John 1:7) then must selflessly pursue whatever it is that God shows him to do, "as the [servant] of Christ, doing the will of God from the heart" (Eph. 6:6). Wholehearted engagement in the will of God pleases Him. Then, the child of God is to give thanks in everything, "for this is the will of God in Christ Jesus concerning you" (I Thess. 5:18).

It "is the will of God, that with well doing ye may put to silence the ignorance of foolish men" (I Pet. 2:15). In cases of persecution or criticism, "it is better, if the will of God be so, that [one] suffer for well doing" (3:17) than it would be to suffer for having done wrong. The ultimate goal of avoiding the be-yourself rebellion so common in our day is "that ye may stand perfect and complete in all the will of God" (Col. 4:12); that is, for Christ and His will to be all that the believer needs (no lacks) and wants (no lusts). A be-yourself rebel can never know even a smidgen of such fulfillment and contentment, but "whosoever shall do the will of God, the same is my brother, and my sister, and mother" (Mark 3:35); and "he that doeth the will of God abideth for ever" (I John 2:17).

The Circle and the Railing

The Lord drew me a circle, a circle big and wide;
He then gave me commandment and bid me stay inside
Within its bounds of safety, but I would not abide.
I tiptoed to the circle, and in and out I went.
No harm just then befell me, no blight, no detriment;
No trouble came to haunt me, so I was well content.
The Lord put up a railing, a railing strong and stout;
He then gave me a warning and charged me not to scout
Beyond its line of refuge, but rules I always flout.
I climbed upon the railing, and from it I did spring.
No difficulty touched me, no bane, no suffering;
No burden lit upon me; of life I was the king.
The Lord erased my circle, took down my boundary rail;
His Word no more enjoined me nor urged me not to fail.
I sensed an eerie freedom like calm before a gale.
My freedom turned to daring, to foolish self-reliance,
To insolent immunity and arrogant defiance.
The Lord had let me have my way; I stood among the giants!
The Lord sent down a tempest, a tempest harsh and bold;
He then gave me a chiding, a scolding stern and cold,
About my haughty slackness toward what I'd been told.
I searched for God's wide circle, His railing, His entreat.
No hiding place enclosed me, no shelter, no retreat;
No guiding voice assured me; I loathed my proud conceit.
God drew another circle, another railing raised;
He then gave admonition; into my eyes He gazed
With resolute insistence that left me awed, amazed.
I stay inside this circle, behind this railing stand—
No prison, but a haven, a fort, a promised land.
And now I'm in submission, and He is in command.

—Jeff Farnham

Glossary

A rebel is identified by many words. Aside from the expository analysis of Ezekiel 2:1–10 in chapter 1, and in addition to the examples given in the ensuing chapters, it is helpful to the student of Scripture, as well as to the reader of this book, to understand that God employs several words to identify separate details of rebel thinking and rebel activity. While it is not important to list every individual word, it is advantageous to possess a general comprehension of biblical words that are associated with rebellion. In an age where sins are renamed for comfort and appeasement, every believer needs a refresher course to remind him who really is a rebel and how the God of Scripture views his rebellion.

All words have an actual meaning, an underlying innuendo and a normal contextual usage. The word *rebel* in any of its various noun, verb, adjective or adverb forms has a negative connotation. In the context of this book, it refers primarily to rebellion against God and any God-ordained earthly authority. A rebel is a person who exalts his thinking against God and then embarks upon a lifestyle, a mission, if you please, with that anti-God agenda foremost in his thinking.

Abomination (n.); abominabl(e)(y) (adj., adv.) In scores of cases, the Word of God uses this term to identify that which is disgusting and detestable to God. No question exists as to the wrongness and unrighteousness of anything that God calls an abomination; therefore, God's bold summary statement in

Deuteronomy 25:16 is both appropriate and powerful: "For all that do such things, and all that do unrighteously, are an abomination unto the LORD thy God." A rebel does such things as God condemns and bans. A rebel does unrighteously, committing acts that are unjust and immoral. It follows then, that a rebel is an abomination to the God of authority because he engages in prohibited acts spawned in a mind of perverted attitudes.

Evildoer (n.) This word is a general term covering a broad spectrum. Essentially, an evildoer is one whose doings are defined by God as evil (not good) because said doings are wrong and bad in the clear judgment of God. Since the Lord denounced rebellion as akin to "witchcraft," one can easily categorize rebels as evildoers (I Sam. 15:23). Second Chronicles 12:14 says of Rehoboam that "he did evil, because he prepared not his heart to seek the LORD," and Rehoboam was most definitely rebellious against the Lord God of his fathers.

Fool (n.); foolish(ly) (n., adj., adv.) The Holy Ghost uses this word nearly one hundred forty times, including several references to "the foolish" as a group of people. This word conveys the overall and obvious idea of the absence of wisdom. The specific categories of fools in Scripture include the uninstructed fool who has not learned and the uninterested fool who will not learn. The latter is more a rebel than the former because he "refuse[s] and rebel[s]" (Isa. 1:20), but all the fools of Scripture are rebels to a degree. The uninstructed have passively resisted the law written within their hearts, and the uninterested have added to that passive resistance an active rejection of the truths of God that have been spoken in their ears.

Froward (n., adj.) Twenty-one times the Bible uses this word, which means "crooked, bent, not straight." Any person who has bent the clear, straight truths of God to accommodate his perverted lifestyle or to mollify his wretchedness is in rebellion.

Pervert (v.); perverse (n., adj.) Appearing in its variant forms over forty times, this word connotes one who has wrestled and forced his way against the plain teaching of God to the point of profaning the way of God altogether. This the rebel has done, often through the use of great force and with grave consequences. With good reason then, Proverbs 19:1 tells us, "Better is the poor that walketh in his integrity, than he that is perverse in his lips, and is a fool."

Rebel (n., v.); rebellion (n.); rebellious (n., adj.) This word can hardly escape mention in a book entitled as this one is. The most common appearance of this word is in the books of the prophets in their denunciation of Israel. Basic to the idea of this word is opposition to God and His command; for instance, as God says in Numbers 20:24: "Ye rebelled against my word at the water of Meribah." Rebels literally rise up and oppose the authority of God, whether that authority is vested in God Himself or in His divinely appointed leaders. Scripture uses a form of this word nearly one hundred times. God's summation is that "the rebellious dwell in a dry land" (Ps. 68:6) because the refreshing showers of the Lord do not come to them.

Scoffer (n.) God mentions the scoffer only once, in II Peter 3:3, where the plural is used. A scoffer's response to God is "Bah, humbug!" or "Pshaw!" and is exemplified in the attitudes of many within God's Word.

Scorn (n., v.) scorner (n.) In its very sound and pronunciation, this word communicates what its definition and connotation convey. A scorner is one who scoffs at instruction and sneers at correction. The sinful characteristics that accompany scorn include the hatred of knowledge, the hatred of the wise reprover, the refusal to hear any rebuke, pride and haughtiness, strife and contention, and the inability to find any true wisdom. No wonder Proverbs 24:9 states that "the scorner is an abomination to men."

Sinner (n.) This word and its plural appear nearly seventy times in God's Word. This term has both positional and practical meaning. Positionally, the sinner is an unsaved person, still dead in trespasses and sins, and so named because sin is his nature. Practically speaking, a sinner is one who commits sin, even though the Bible does not use this word to refer to a believer who sins. God gives many specific names to sinners— idolators, boasters, blasphemers, fornicators, murderers, etc.— but occasionally He resorts to the all-encompassing generalization "sinner." To cite one who fights against God and call him a sinner is not hasty judgment; rather, it is righteous and wise judgment. Rebels are sinners.

Strange (adj.) Occurring nearly eighty times, this word is often used to communicate the idea of "idolatrous" or "immoral." The strange woman and the evil man are subjects of scathing, judicial condemnation in Proverbs because of their danger to any who wish to follow God. One who studies rebellion for any length of time will conclude that rebellion is idolatry because rebellion sets up another god and dethrones the true God. This same research will demonstrate that a rebel is spiritually immoral, having departed from the true Lover of his soul while pursuing and engaging another lover.

Transgressor (n.); transgression (n.); transgress (v.) The various forms of this word are found over one hundred fifty times in the Bible. A transgressor is a rebel because, after God establishes boundaries of acceptable character and action, the transgressor purposely steps across those boundaries. The two words *transgressor* and *rebel* are associated in Ezekiel 2:3, where God said to Ezekiel, "I send thee to…a rebellious nation that hath…transgressed against me, even unto this very day."

Unrighteous (n., adj.) Although this word is found only

nine times in Scripture, it is significant both as an adjective and as a collective noun. The basic meaning is one who has not been made right or just through the blood of Christ. He is unsaved and, therefore, unrighteous. By honest application, any rebel is unrighteous, whether saved or unsaved, because even if the rebel has found justification by faith in Christ, his actions are still the unrighteous works of the flesh and the world at the behest of the god of this world, Satan.

Wicked (n., adj.); wickedly (adv.) These two terms are used nearly three hundred fifty times in God's Word, and they can be descriptive or collective, identifying a group whose actions and attitudes are opposed to God. For any person to rise up and adopt a premise or assume a position opposed to God is certainly wicked; for that person to pursue said premises and positions to the point of practice is the full expression of wickedness. Rebellious people are wicked before God and men. Job spoke of "those that rebel against the light" and who "know not the ways thereof, nor abide in the paths thereof" (24:13). Even a cursory reading of that passage shows that the rebels to whom he refers were wicked people.

For a complete list of books available from the Sword of the Lord, write to Sword of the Lord Publishers, P.O. Box 1099, Murfreesboro, Tennessee 37133.

(800) 24-SWORD
(FAX (615) 278-1309
www.swordofthelord.com